COMBAT AIRCRAFT

135 A-7 CORSAIR II UNITS 1975-91

SERIES EDITOR TONY HOLMES

135 COMBAT AIRCRAFT

Peter B Mersky with Mike Crutch and Tony Holmes

A-7 CORSAIR II UNITS 1975-91

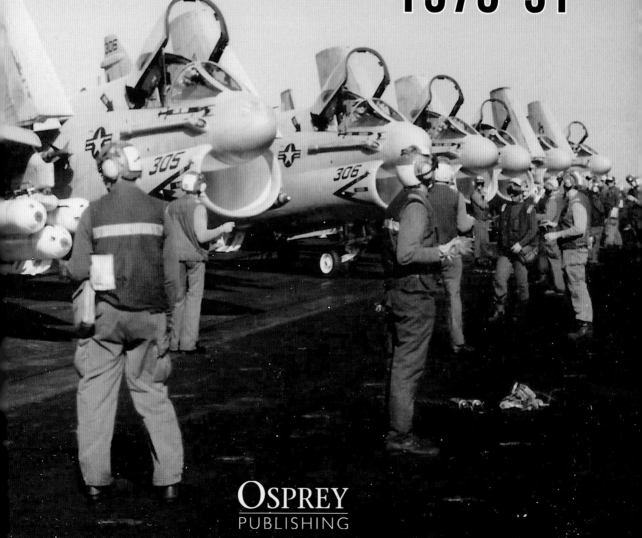

OSPREY
PUBLISHING

OSPREY PUBLISHING
Bloomsbury Publishing Plc
PO Box 883, Oxford, OX1 9PL, UK
1385 Broadway, 5th Floor, New York, NY 10018, USA
E-mail: info@ospreypublishing.com
www.ospreypublishing.com

OSPREY is a trademark of Osprey Publishing Ltd

First published in Great Britain in 2021

A catalogue record for this book is available from the British Library.

ISBN: PB 9781472840639; eBook 9781472840646;
ePDF 9781472840615; XML 9781472840622

21 22 23 24 25 10 9 8 7 6 5 4 3 2 1

Edited by Tony Holmes
Cover Artwork by Gareth Hector
Aircraft Profiles by Jim Laurier
Index by Fionbar Lyons
Originated by PDQ Digital Media Solutions, UK
Printed and bound in India by Replika Press Private Ltd

Osprey Publishing supports the Woodland Trust, the UK's leading woodland conservation charity.

To find out more about our authors and books visit **www.ospreypublishing.com**. Here you will find extracts, author interviews, details of forthcoming events and the option to sign up for our newsletter.

Front Cover
Two weeks after the communist takeover of Saigon on 30 April 1975, armed conflict again pulled American forces into the area with the capture of the US-flagged container ship SS *Mayaguez* in international waters. The Cambodian renegades who seized the vessel anchored it off Koh Tang. The captors' intentions were unclear, and President Gerald R Ford was now faced with the prospect of sending American troops and weapons into battle again. The closest aircraft carrier was the veteran USS *Coral Sea* (CVA-43) and its air wing, CVW-15.

Although the Cambodians released *Mayaguez*, they held onto its crew. This prompted the Ford administration to authorise CVW-15 to mount a series of strikes against Cambodian military targets from 1000 hrs on 15 May. A-7E Corsair IIs and A-6A Intruders targeted Ream Field, which was home to both armed T-28s and MiG-17s – types which could oppose US troops, and the helicopters trying to insert them into a contested landing site.

VA-22 XO Cdr Al Dundon led five A-7s against the airport, each Corsair II carrying six Mk 82 500-lb bombs and two Mk 20 Rockeye bomblet canisters. Lt(jg) Mark Sloat, flying A-7E BuNo 158005, was in the No 2 position as they heard a USAF pilot call he had spotted a boat containing people waving a white flag. It was the *Mayaguez* crew. Nevertheless, the A-7 pilots prepared for their delivery runs. Avoiding enemy flak, they each dropped their bombs and then swung around for a second pass to deliver their Rockeyes, each weapon opening 500 ft above the ground. Lt(jg) Sloat's ordnance hit a large aircraft, possibly a transport, parked on the ramp and it burst into flames. The accuracy of his delivery prompted a call of 'Nice hit' over the radio by his squadronmate, Lt Ed Fahy.

After an aborted strafing run that saw his Mk 61 cannon fail to fire, Lt(jg) Sloat pulled off the target and held over an offshore island, prior to rejoining his division on the return flight to their ship (*Cover artwork by Gareth Hector*)

Previous Pages
A-7Es from both VA-46 and VA-72 have been manned and sit with their engines idling on the bow of USS *John F Kennedy* (CV-67) ready for their next mission during Operation *Desert Storm*. The aircraft in the foreground are armed with Mk 20 Rockeye canisters on triple ejector pylons, as well as cheek-mounted AIM-9Ls (*US Navy*)

CONTENTS

INTRODUCTION

For a young Naval Aviator, nothing is as wonderful as flying his fleet aircraft in a challenging environment, testing both himself and his mount to the edge of their capabilities. For Lt Mark I Fox in his VA-72 A-7E Corsair II, the challenge of flying high speed at low altitude – hundreds of feet *below* the rim of 'Star Wars Canyon' in Oman – was as great a prospect as anyone could hope for.

In April 1983, Mark 'MRT' Fox was an experienced, second cruise lieutenant with 1000 hours in his log book, 800 of them in the Corsair II. Launching from USS *America* (CV-66), the 1978 Annapolis graduate from Abilene, Texas, was at the top of his game. Over the previous six weeks, he and his air wing (CVW-1) had been flying in a series of bilateral US–Omani military exercises called *Beacon Flash*, and operating over Oman's varied terrain had become very familiar. Facing experienced former RAF pilots of the Sultan of Oman's Air Force (SOAF) flying British-built Jaguar S(O)s in these exercises was both challenging and rewarding.

In particular, Oman's topography varied from absolutely flat desert to extremely rugged and mountainous terrain. One river formed a canyon that resembled a shorter and smaller version of the Grand Canyon, with its rim more than 1000 ft above the dried riverbed below. When they initially flew through the canyon, the air wing's aviators took a conservative 'stay at the canyon rim' approach that only required mild manoeuvring. As time passed, experience and familiarity with the canyon grew, resulting

One of Cdr John 'Lites' Leenhouts' unique photographs gives a good idea of the close confines of 'Star Wars Canyon' in Saudi Arabia as he manoeuvres his A-7 through its tricky sandstone terrain during Operation *Desert Shield* in 1990. The similarly nicknamed canyon in Oman was also frequently flown through by US Navy pilots, including then-Lt Mark Fox, operating from carriers in the Arabian Sea (*US Navy*)

Lt Mark Fox of VA-72 in March 1983. Note what is written on the name tag sewn onto his flight suit – *CORSAIR PILOT (US Navy)*

in more aggressive flying at lower altitudes. A 'one-way' flow to the sea rule was also established to eliminate potential mid-air collisions. The air wing dubbed it 'Star Wars Canyon', and flying through it was just pure fun. Midway through the canyon, the riverbed made a right 90-degree turn followed by a left 90-degree turn, with essentially vertical granite walls in the lower parts of the serpentine twist. A 'camelback' rock formation on the right provided a way to avoid the narrow lower riverbed 'S-bend' turn.

After much study, and many flights through the canyon (*over* the 'camelback' cut-through), Fox realised there was enough room for an A-7 to negotiate the twisting path, and he finally – and carefully – flew his jet *through* the 'S-bend' in the lower part of the riverbed. It demanded thoughtful preparation and total concentration, but it was exhilarating. On this particular day, the mission was by now old hat: launch from the ship, go 'feet dry' (ingress) into central Oman, fly a low-level navigation route over the flat desert, drop practice bombs in a pop-up attack on a SOAF target and, still flying at low altitude, go 'feet wet' (egress) via 'Star Wars Canyon' and return to the ship.

The mission was executed exactly according to the brief. As 'Dash-3' in a three-aircraft formation, Fox put his practice bombs directly on target and then dropped back into single file to fly through the canyon prior to going 'feet wet'. Carefully avoiding the jet wash of the two Corsair IIs ahead of him, Fox unconsciously accelerated as he descended on his approach to the canyon 'S-bend'. The challenge of threading his jet between those granite walls beckoned, but he was confident he could make it through – he had done it 24 hours earlier at 350 knots, although now he was heading for the 'S-bend' at about 450 knots.

As soon as he committed to flying through the lower canyon he realised that things were *not* the same as yesterday. 'Oh man', he thought to himself, 'I'm going more than 100 knots faster'. He felt a 'shot of cold ammonia' hit his heart. The turn radius at this speed was too great for him to negotiate the upcoming 90-degree turn. He could not slow down, and there was no way to escape what was coming. 'I'm dead!' he thought. However, Fox was a highly capable young Naval Aviator (as his later career would prove). He made what he called a 'knife-edge' turn along the 'grey-brown granite wall', pulling g, with his A-7 shuddering and his muscles tensed.

Then, suddenly, the first wall flashed under his nose and he reversed his turn into a left 90-degree angle of bank to avoid the second canyon wall, again pulling hard to stay in the riverbed. Manoeuvring hard into the two Reno-racing-style 'knife-edge' turns had slowed the Corsair II down sufficiently enough to negotiate the 'S-bend' canyon. Safely through the latter, Fox started a climb out of the canyon. It was at this point he was stunned to see his knees uncontrollably shaking as his A-7 gained precious altitude.

Subsequently rejoining his flight over the water as they headed back to the ship, it would take Fox some time to regain his composure as he flew in the direction of his carrier. For the remainder of his flight he recalled his near-death experience over and over again in his head, pondering how close he had come to killing himself in a perfectly good A-7E. Among other things, Fox's string of eight OK-graded three-wire landings ended with a fair one-wire. Nevertheless, he was glad to have returned in one piece, along with his trusty Corsair II.

Fox later described the incident in an article for *Approach* (the Naval Aviation Safety Review), ending his submission with the line 'I have only the A-7's magnificent ability to dissipate energy to thank for my life (and a benevolent God, who looks out for fools and Naval Aviators)'.

Lt Fox had a stellar career that saw him fly many combat missions in the Middle East and undertake service in a wide variety of leadership roles that culminated in him attaining the rank of Vice Admiral. Among his military awards are the Silver Star, the Defense Distinguished Service Medal, the Navy Distinguished Service Medal with gold star (indicating two awards), Legion of Merit with two gold stars, and the Distinguished Flying Cross with Combat V.

Lt Fox was flying 'Decoy 407' (BuNo 160550) on the day he had his close shave in 'Star Wars Canyon'. The aircraft is seen here during the early stages of VA-72's 1982-83 deployment with CVW-1 embarked in USS *America* (CV-66). Both A-7Es are carrying empty TERs, and 'Decoy 402' is also equipped with a AN/AAR-45 FLIR pod (*US Navy*)

Author's Note

Many people from several services offered their help with photographs and first-hand accounts of flying the A-7 during the period covered in this book, for which I am very grateful. Unless otherwise noted, their service is the US Navy. If I have left out anyone, please accept my apologies. I would like to thank;

Cdr Hugh Alcock, Timothy Bostic (Navy History and Heritage Command (NHHC)), Rear Admiral Jerry Breast, Capt Lawrence Brennan, Vice Admiral Herb Browne, Rear Admiral John Calvert, Capt Jeffrey Cathey, Capt Carl W 'Tad' Chamberlain, Aviation Fire Control Technician Airman Len Chatham, Tom Chee, Capt Dave Dollarhide, Admiral Mark Fitzgerald, Vice Admiral Mark Fox, Lt Cdr Tom Ganse, Lt Mat Garretson, Lt Col Robert M Gatewood (USAF), Lt Jeff Greer, Col Christopher Holmes (USAF), Photographer's Mate, Second Class Kenneth Jack, Sarah Jeffery (Martin-Baker Aircraft Company), Lt Dave Johnson, Capt Leslie Kappel, Capt Dean Koehler, Rear Admiral James Lair, Dr Christopher Lamb (US Navy), Capt John Leenhouts, Capt George Lundy, Michael Maus (Deputy Public Affairs Officer, COMNAVAIRLANT), Vice Admiral John Mazach, Alecia Midgett, Lt Cdr Rick Morgan, Holly Reed (Joint History Office, Joint Chiefs of Staff), Capt Brett Reicher (US Army), Michael Rhodes (NHHC), Lt David Schneiderman, Lt Mark Sloat, Gabrielle Spiers (NHHC), Cdr Don Stanton, Yeoman, Second Class Wayne Stewart, Maj Robert Thomas (USAF Reserve), Shawn Vreeland (Joint History Office, Joint Chiefs of Staff), Col Ralph Wetterhahn (USAF) and Capt Kent White.

The authors acknowledge the use of quotes in the *Desert Shield/Storm* chapter from the outstanding PSL book *Iron Hand – Smashing the Enemy's Air Defences* by Anthony M Thornborough and Frank B Mormillo.

CHAPTER ONE

THE LAST BATTLE?

USS *Coral Sea* (CVA-43) sails at speed off the coast of Cambodia during mid-May 1975, with aircraft from CVW-15 chained down around the edge of the flightdeck. Eight A-7Es from VA-22 and VA-94 are lined up over bow catapult one (*US Navy*)

Much was expected of the tough-looking little attack jet when the first A-7 Corsair IIs and their squadron, VA-147, joined CVW-2 aboard USS *Ranger* (CVA-61) in December 1967 for the new aircraft's maiden combat cruise to Vietnam. The jet was scheduled to expeditiously replace the US Navy's A-4 Skyhawk in light attack squadrons within both the Pacific and Atlantic Fleets, the Douglas aircraft having borne the brunt of carrier-based attack missions in the wake of the unexpected Gulf of Tonkin Incident in August 1964. By the time the Paris Peace Accords came into effect on 27 January 1973, ending the US military's direct involvement in the Vietnam War, only one carrier, USS *Hancock* (CVA-19), still included the A-4 in its air wing.

The A-7 rapidly equipped most of the US Navy's light attack squadrons, although the A-4 lingered on with several Naval Air Reserve units. The 1968 recall of reserve squadrons because of the so-called Pueblo Crisis, when North Korea captured the intelligence ship USS *Pueblo* (AGER-2) on 23 January 1968, was less than successful and resulted in a major reorganisation of the reserve into more of a mirror image of a frontline carrier air wing. This also included re-equipping reserve squadrons with more modern, fleet-compatible aircraft such as Corsair IIs. A-7A/Bs subsequently saw long reserve service, although from the early 1970s most fleet squadrons, but not all, flew the A-7E. Indeed, CVW-5, forward-deployed to Japan in 1973 and embarked in USS *Midway* (CVA-41) when at sea, included two squadrons (VA-56 and VA-93) that retained A-model Corsair IIs until 1977. CVW-19, assigned to *Midway's* sister-ship USS *Franklin D Roosevelt* (CV-42), boasted no fewer than three squadrons (VA-153, VA-155 and VA-215) equipped with A-7Bs when it participated in the carrier's final cruise, to the Mediterranean, in 1976-77.

THE END IN VIETNAM

Returning to the conflict in Southeast Asia in January 1973, although the peace accords had ushered in a ceasefire, carriers remained on patrol off *Yankee Station* as US forces kept a weather eye on North Vietnam. Operation *End Sweep* also sent minesweeper CH-53A helicopters into North Vietnam's harbours to clear the mines dropped in the last months of the conflict, while prisoners of war, many of whom had spent five to seven arduous years in captivity, began their long but happy trip home.

From 28 January – the first day of the ceasefire – USS *Oriskany* (CVA-34) and USS *Constellation* (CVA-64) launched strikes into Laos, as did USS *Enterprise* (CVAN-65) and USS *Ranger* (CVA-61) from 11 February, against 'lines-of-communication'. The latter were trails being used by the North Vietnamese to send supplies to communist fighters in Laos. The fine point here was that the Laotian government had requested the strikes, which meant that they did not contravene the ceasefire. This effectively meant that the war in Southeast Asia was continuing even as the US government endeavoured to extricate its forces from South Vietnam and thus hopefully bring the long-running war to some kind of a halt.

The Paris Peace Accords did indeed bring direct US involvement in the Vietnamese conflict to an end. However, Southeast Asia was still 'hot', with periodic skirmishes breaking out in neighbouring Laos and Cambodia between communist factions and government forces trying to maintain the shaky peace. By March 1975, plans were being made to evacuate American and other workers from the troubled peninsula. On 12 April, Operation *Eagle Pull* was activated to extract US citizens and allied Cambodians from the country, and the Marines were sent in to establish a perimeter around the capital, Phnom Penh.

Seven days later, Operation *Frequent Wind* commenced as American civilians and key South Vietnamese personnel were flown out, especially from the capital, Saigon. North Vietnamese forces were rapidly rolling south to finish the incomplete invasion of the southern half of the divided country, cut short by the ceasefire in January 1973. By 25 April the North Vietnamese Army was firmly in control of both Saigon and South Vietnam.

US carriers orbited offshore, their aircraft (both *Hancock* and *Midway* had temporarily beached their air wings and were now operating exclusively as helicopter carriers) and crews standing by ready to protect the constant 'aerial bridge' of helicopters and aircraft that shuttled back and forth from the embattled South Vietnamese cities carrying thousands of refugees fleeing their war-torn country to an uncertain future. Aircraft from *Coral Sea* (VA-22 and VA-94 embarked) and *Enterprise* (VA-27 and VA-97 embarked) flew a total of 173 sorties – 44 of them by the two A-7E squadrons of CVW-14, embarked in CVAN-65. The US Navy units covered 638 flights by USAF and US Marine Corps fixed-wing aircraft

The US-flagged container ship SS *Mayaguez* sits at anchor near Koh Tang after being seized by Cambodian naval personnel of the communist Khmer Rouge on 12 May 1975. This photograph was taken by a USAF aircraft (possibly a Thailand-based F-111) shortly after the vessel had been boarded (*USAF*)

and 250 CIA helicopter flights evacuating 395 Americans and 4475 South Vietnamese from Tan Son Nhut Air Base on the outskirts of Saigon. Other evacuation missions took 978 Americans and 1120 South Vietnamese and allied nationals from Saigon itself. In fact, a *Coral Sea* A-7 from VA-22 had escorted the last helicopter – a US Marine Corps CH-46 Sea Knight of HMM-165 – from the US embassy, carrying out American Ambassador Graham Martin and his family, on the morning of 30 April.

Two weeks after the communist takeover in Saigon, a combined US Navy, US Marine Corps and USAF operation that spanned three days would result in the final injuries, fatalities and aircraft losses in-theatre. On 12 May, Cambodian naval personnel of the communist Khmer Rouge faction that now ruled the country boarded the US-flagged container ship SS *Mayaguez* in international waters and had its crew anchor the vessel off Tang Island (often incorrectly referred to as Koh Tang Island ('Koh' means 'island' in Cambodian). The captors' intentions were initially unclear, and President Gerald R Ford was faced with his first international crisis.

There was concern about a lack of US support for South Vietnam as it was being overrun by the invading North Vietnamese, indicating to neighbouring countries a loss of American strength and resolve in the region. While the situation was rapidly developing, aircraft carriers and other potential sources of aid were assembling in Southeast Asia in readiness for a call to arms. One of the ships in the area was *Coral Sea*, which had left Alameda, California, in December 1974 with CVW-15 embarked. As previously noted, amongst the air wing's squadrons were A-7E-equipped VA-22 and VA-94, and VA-95 with its A-6A/KA-6D Intruders. Many of CVW-15's aircrew and enlisted personnel had seen previous combat deployments to the region prior to the 1973 ceasefire. However, with the recently instituted end to the fighting, there was no certainty that air power would be used to solve the *Mayaguez* Incident.

US Navy assets had been monitoring events since the ship's capture. Primary among them were crews of several P-3B Orions, the US Navy's foremost maritime patrol aircraft. They offered lengthy loiter times for watching such proceedings. An aircraft from VP-17, deployed to NAS Cubi Point, in the Philippines, to assist VP-4 because of the huge size of the area of responsibility shared by maritime patrols squadrons, sent initial intelligence that had alerted senior US Navy commands in the region. The Orion crews had to be cautious as the Cambodians were known to have well-armed gunboats fitted with 20 mm and 40 mm anti-aircraft artillery (AAA) weapons. They had, in fact, downed a P-3B from VP-26, temporarily based at U-Tapao, Thailand, on 1 April 1968, killing all 12 crew.

On 13 May another P-3 crew from VP-17 had observed *Mayaguez* with two Cambodian gunboats tied up alongside. The gunboat crews fired on

the Orion as it flew down the port side of the container ship, hitting the aircraft in the vertical tail with one 0.50-calibre round. Considering the damage superficial, the aircraft's commander decided to remain on station. The ship then got underway, seemingly heading for a nearby port. However, as it sailed past Koh Tang, it turned into a cove on the north coast of the island and anchored about a mile offshore.

As the P-3 crew now loitered nearby, keeping watch on the hijacked ship, USAF F-111s, F-4s and A-7s appeared overhead. The Orion crews now shifted their attention to looking for Cambodian naval units, finding several gunboats (and fishing craft) in the immediate vicinity.

The following day (14 May), a trawler similar to the one initially thought to have taken the crew of *Mayaguez* into Koh Tang harbour 24 hours earlier was spotted by a P-3. The aircraft made a low pass over the boat and 'Caucasians' were seen huddled in the bow. USAF aircraft, including an AC-130 gunship, subsequently made close passes on the trawler, which maintained its course into the foggy interior of Kompong Som harbour. It was now assumed that *Mayaguez*'s crew was in Cambodia, although this could not be confirmed. US commands up to the White House and President Ford were relatively in the dark as to how to proceed. As they had done for the last decade, American aircrew dutifully prepared to follow orders as strike plans were sent out.

At dawn on 15 May, a combined effort to free the captured ship and search parts of Koh Tang for the crew began when aircraft and helicopters were manned for missions against the island and Ream Field (now Sihanouk International Airport), on the coast of Cambodia. Armed T-28 trainers and MiG-17 fighter-bombers of the Air Force of the Khmer Liberation Army were based at the latter site, and it was feared that both types could

The pilot of VA-22's 'Beefsteak 305' unfolds the wings of his aircraft as the jet is marshalled towards CVA-43's bow catapults in early 1975. The A-7E has 25-lb Mk 76 practice bombs attached to its starboard underwing TER, these weapons being used to simulate the ballistics of Mk 82 500-lb low drag general purpose bombs. The VA-94 aircraft under tow has just returned from a training sortie *(US Navy)* inflict heavy casualties on US troops inserted during the operation. It soon became obvious that the mission would be fiercely opposed by the Cambodian military when USAF CH-53s and HH-53s sustained hits from heavy ground fire, wounding a number of Marines within the helicopters, as they approached Koh Tang.

Shortly after the Marines had landed, an orbiting P-3 crew spotted what turned out to be the trawler with all 40 crewmen from *Mayaguez* on board and on their way to be released. With this news, the Marines were ordered to withdraw. Intense enemy fire made the extraction difficult, and USS *Henry B Wilson* (DDG-7) and USS *Harold E Holt* (FF-1074) had to provide support, as did several flights of aircraft from *Coral Sea* – A-6s and A-7s from the carrier were tasked with attacking Ream Field.

STRIKING BACK AT THE KHMER ROUGE

As soon as *Coral Sea* was within range of Cambodia on 15 May combat flight operations began. The Cambodians were very much aware of the building threat posed by US military aircraft, ships and men. The main 'weapon' would be the aircraft from *Coral Sea* in a series of three strikes that included A-7s from VA-22 and VA-94 and A-6 Intruders from VA-95. The question was whether and when to launch. At first, the word was for the aircraft not to drop their ordnance or to go to Kompong Som harbour. Soon the decision was flashed to cancel the strikes altogether even after USAF helicopters had been shot down and Marines were fighting for their lives when engaged by unexpectedly heavy opposition ashore on Koh Tang.

The Cambodians had released the ship, but evidently not the crew, who were apparently now huddled in the bow of a Thai fishing trawler somewhere offshore of Koh Tang. Finally, President Ford gave permission to launch the strikes. By 0845 hrs the first wave of aircraft had departed *Coral Sea* and were over their targets. But another Flash message from the Joint Chiefs of Staff stopped the mission and the strikers had to drop their ordnance in the sea before returning to the carrier. Communication from Washington, D.C. and field commands continued to confuse matters until a second strike was launched at 1000 hrs to bomb Ream Field.

The lack of specific planning and orders from higher command plagued a smooth launch and strike, as had been the case throughout the Vietnam War. Although Cdr (later Rear Admiral) Jack Calvert, CO of VA-22, had quickly learned of the capture of *Mayaguez* on 12 May, by 0800 hrs on the 15th he had still not received orders to launch against the Cambodians. The status of the ship and its crew was only now filtering in largely through the good work done by the P-3s and their crews. Finally, shortly after 0800 hrs, Cdr Calvert and his squadron operations officer, Lt Cdr (later Rear Admiral) Jim Lair, launched as part of a four-jet flight of A-7s. Incredibly, they had no assigned targets. Once

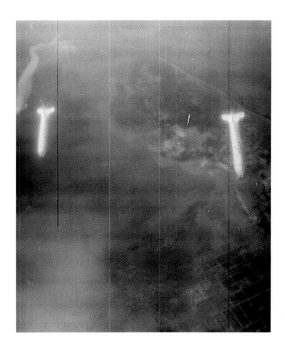

Taken by the A-7's belly-mounted KB-18 bomb damage assessment camera, which operated automatically when the ordnance was 'pickled' (the pilot had no additional control over the camera), this photograph shows Lt(jg) Mark Sloat's Mk 20 Rockeye bomblets hitting a Cambodian aircraft. The camera took only black-and-white photographs (*US Navy*)

in the vicinity of Koh Tang, the Corsair II pilots were held in a holding orbit due to the airspace being occupied by USAF F-4s from Thailand.

At this time, USAF Special Operations CH-53 helicopters arrived to insert Marines on Koh Tang, only to be shot down with heavy casualties by Khmer Rouge AAA. The confusion prevented the US Navy A-7s from attacking enemy positions, and after some 90 minutes, Cdr Calvert took his frustrated pilots back to *Coral Sea* after dropping their ordnance in the water. Meanwhile, the crews of VA-95's A-6s had launched on a mission to attack Ream Field. However, a 1000 hrs launch of four more A-7s from VA-22 and another 'tag-along' VA-94 Corsair II reached the airport first. The XO of VA-22, Cdr Al Dundon, was leading the five A-7s, each of which was armed with six Mk 82 500-lb bombs and two Mk 20 Rockeye canisters (the latter carrying 247 bomblets – an effective destructive weapon against runways).

As the Corsair IIs approached the target, a USAF pilot radioed he had spotted a boat with people and a white flag, which was in fact the crew of the *Mayaguez*. Nevertheless, the A-7s lined up for their bomb delivery. AAA engaged the jets, whose pilots resorted to mild jinking to avoid the Cambodian fire. Each of the pilots dropped their Mk 82 bombs on the runway and then swung around for a second pass to deliver their two Rockeye canisters, which opened some 500 ft above the ground to release their bomblets. Lt(jg) Mark Sloat was flying in the No 2 position of the five-aircraft formation, and his ordnance hit a dispersal area as he rolled to the left to watch the impact. A large aircraft, possibly a C-47 transport, burst into flames, and his squadronmate Lt Ed Fahy called 'Nice hit!' over the radio.

Having expended all of their underwing ordnance, the *Coral Sea's* Corsair II pilots set up a strafing pattern to hit other aircraft in runway revetments. Lt(jg) Sloat rolled into a 15-degree strafing angle, but his aircraft's single Mk 61 20 mm cannon would not fire. Frustrated, he called the XO, who told him to pull off and orbit overhead a nearby island offshore, where they would pick him up as they headed back to the ship.

Meanwhile, the VA-95 A-6s, which had also attacked the airfield, and were now going 'feet wet' back to the carrier, got a sharp radio call from an irritated USAF controller demanding to know who had authorised the US Navy strike on the airfield. By then, of course, it was too late to abort the Ream Field attack, or another strike at around 1100 hrs that resulted in the sinking of a Cambodian gunboat by an A-7.

Lt Cdr Jim Lair from VA-22 leads in A-7Es from both his unit and VA-94 in an attack on a Cambodian PBR. The white 'puffs' visible behind the aircraft came from the initial drop of Mk 20 Rockeye canisters, which missed the fast-moving boat. Moments later Lair sunk the PBR with a well-aimed burst of 20 mm cannon fire (*US Navy*)

VA-22's Lt Ed Fahy, Lt Cdr Bob Swartz, Cdr Al Dundon and Lt(jg) Mark Sloat carried out the attack on Ream Field. They are seen here standing by an aircraft probably on the day after the strike, but which carries a load similar to that on their A-7s on 15 May – six 500-lb Mk 82 bombs on two TERs and a pair of Mk 20 Rockeye cluster bombs. This jet is also armed with at least one 1000-lb Mk 83 (*US Navy*)

The aircraft involved in the latter mission were flown by Lt Cdr Lair, his wingman Lt Kirk Lewis (also from VA-22) and Lt Jay Munninghoff from VA-94. Their pre-launch briefing had included details on the insertion of the Marines by CH-53s and the direction to check in with the USAF Airborne Battlefield Command and Control Center (ABCCC) EC-130E that was monitoring the action on Koh Tang. The Carrier Air Wing commander, then Cdr (later Rear Admiral) E I 'Hoagy' Carmichael, flying a VA-95 A-6, had spotted a fast-moving former US Navy patrol boat, riverine (PBR), that had been captured by the Khmer Rouge earlier in the year headed toward *Mayaguez*. At this time, no word had reached the air wing about the release of the ship's crew and their return to *Mayaguez*.

When the A-7s arrived overhead the PBR, which was estimated to be moving at 25 knots, Lt Cdr Lair and his pilots received clearance from an orbiting EC-130E ABCCC to destroy the boat. At first, the pilots dropped Mk 20 Rockeyes, but due to the boat's speed it outran the bomblets. The PBR was also manoeuvring so aggressively that it complicated the Corsair II pilots' aiming patterns. The only solution was to strafe the enemy vessel, and the A-7's M61 Gatling Gun was perfect for the job. With the capability of firing 4000-6000 rounds per minute (the A-7 carried 1000 rounds of 20 mm ammunition), the M61 could be a devastating weapon, literally sawing its target in half.

Lt Cdr Lair began his strafing run from about 1000 ft in a ten-degree dive angle. 'The in-range firing cue', he recalled, 'appeared on the Heads-Up Display at approximately 700 ft above the water. I started firing and could see the rounds impacting the boat. I ceased firing at approximately 200 ft. I made a hard turn and saw that the boat was sinking. I reported the results and returned to *Coral Sea*'. Two A-6s and six more A-7s, that had also launched at the same time as Lt Cdr Lair, hit an oil refinery, other buildings and warehouses.

When Lair and his flight trapped back aboard, they were briefed that the crew of *Mayaguez* had safely returned to their ship and were preparing to get underway and head to Thailand with their cargo. *Coral Sea*'s aircraft and crews spent the rest of the day monitoring the activities on Koh Tang. That night, the carrier steamed three miles off Koh Tang while Lt(jg) Sloat took his turn strapped into his fully armed A-7 sitting Alert 5 (meaning the jet was capable of being launched in five minutes if required). He was not needed, despite him being able to hear the fighting ashore over the radio in his jet.

The day's operation had seen 289 Marines landed on the island, the release of the *Mayaguez* crew and the ultimate extraction of the Marines and their USAF handlers. Eighteen of the Marines and USAF crews had been killed in action, with the loss of three CH-53s. Three Marines who had been left behind to defend their comrades were subsequently executed by their Khmer Rouge captors.

CAMOUFLAGED CORSAIR IIs

The Corsair IIs from *Coral Sea* were not the only A-7s to see action during the *Mayaguez* Incident, as the USAF's Lt Col R Medley Gatewood (a veteran of earlier Vietnam War combat tours in the F-100 Super Sabre and the A-7D) explains;

'Two squadrons of A-7Ds from the 354th Tactical Fighter Wing (TFW) had deployed to and entered combat from Korat Royal Thai Air Force Base (RTAFB) in September 1972. In addition to the usual attack fighter missions, the A-7s quickly picked up the "Sandy" Combat Search and Rescue Mission, previously perfected by USAF A-1 Skyraiders. By the time I arrived at Korat in June 1974, the general US drawdown had reduced the number of A-7Ds there to just the aircraft assigned to the 3rd Tactical Fighter Squadron (TFS) of the 388th TFW. By the end of April 1975 we had scrambled and supported the evacuations of both Phnom Penh and Saigon. Although we thought that the war was now over, it turned out that there *was* more to come.

'For the "Sandys", it started early on the morning of 13 May. As C Flight commander, I was up early to make sure my flight of four pilots were ready to man our A-7s and assume our turn at dawn-to-dusk "Sandy" alert – a theatre precaution, just in case. We first heard of the possible hijacking of a US container ship in Cambodian waters on the Armed Forces Network Radio as we readied to go to the alert pad. As we headed that way, I thought to myself, "Holy Moly! I wonder what *they* (the all-knowing "they") are going to do about that?" Of course, the first "they" would be us, because we were the only USAF warplanes in-theatre on alert and "loaded for bear"!

'After a hasty briefing by the 388th TFW CO, "Sandy" Flight launched and headed south to the reported location of the container ship *Mayaguez* at a place called Koh Tang. With "Sandys 3" and "4" in a high orbit at 15,000 ft and "Sandy 2" orbiting at 5000 ft, I made several passes at increasingly lower altitudes from different directions over the ship. After spotting no visible movement on the decks or on the bridge, I climbed back up to join up with my No 2. The ship looked to be at anchor, but we took no chances. After a while, we saw smoke building up from the single smoke stack. In order to remind whomever was aboard of our presence, I fired all seven "Willie Pete" 2.75-inch marking rockets from one of my jet's two LAU-32/A pods across the bow. The smoke subsided, and we went back to orbit-and-observe mode.

'Some 20 minutes later, the smoke again began to build from the stack, and I invited my No 2 (a 1st Lieutenant with no combat time as yet) to fire a full pod-load of the marking rockets across the stern of the ship. That put an end to its attempted movement, and we kept watching from 5000 ft until we went bingo fuel and called Nos 3 and 4 to come down and assume on-scene command. Then, we were off in search of a KC-135 tanker. After refuelling, my wingman and I returned to the *Mayaguez* and assumed on-scene command again as the other two A-7s went off to tank up and then return to base.

'As evening approached, a lone F-4D from Udorn RTAFB appeared, checked in with me and offered his only armament (an externally mounted

Alert 'Sandy' Flight A-7D Corsair IIs from the 3rd TFS/388th TFW taxi out at Korat RTAFB after being scrambled on 13 May 1975 by the Seventh Air Force to implement decisions made at the White House and at staff levels. The aircraft is carrying two LAU-32/A pods, each one containing four 'Willie Pete' 2.75-inch marking rockets, on its outboard TER and a CBU-30 tear gas dispenser on station 2. An identical load would have been carried beneath the starboard wing (USAF)

20 mm cannon pod). I told him we had plenty of our own high explosive incendiary if needed, after which he offered to go trolling for us, and I was quite happy to give him a "hell yes" on that concept. Now, in the twilight, we went into a turn 180 degrees apart – the better to keep our trolling buddy in sight. He went straight to work and approached the ship at warp speed at deck-high altitude. And suddenly, out from the edge of the jungle about a mile away from the *Mayaguez,* crossing over the most beautiful white beach you can imagine, in total silence, came a stream of bright red, glowing, "golf ball" sized tracers aimed way behind the trolling F-4. The gunners of this high-calibre machine gun or cannon apparently had never heard of "lead for target motion!" Although it was getting very dark, we got a firm fix on the location of this threat using the "Mark" feature of the A-7D's AN/ASN-91 Navigation/Weapon Delivery Computer and headed home to Korat.

'We were able to give our Intel folks the exact coordinates of that big gun as an Essential Element of Information (EEI), which should have been passed on to any other US units that might be involved in further military operations in the vicinity of Koh Tang. Unfortunately, that EEI was *not* forwarded to at least some of the coming participants. By the time two USAF helicopters tried to put our Marines ashore on that beautiful white beach *two days later,* they ended up directly in the field of fire of that terrible gun, with devastating results. So much for joint planning and operations. To me, the result was the "Mother of All SNAFUs".'

This account is about only the first A-7D mission on the first full day of the *Mayaguez* Incident, and the sortie flown by then Maj Gatewood was more of an intelligence-gathering operation than a rip-roaring combat affair. However, on 14-15 May, there were scores of Corsair II sorties (as well as missions undertaken by USAF Phantom IIs and AC-130 Spectre gunships) flown by the 3rd TFS, most of them involving genuine combat amid the fog of war over what can honestly be described as a chaotic battlefield.

CHAPTER TWO

'PEACE' AFTER VIETNAM

Although US Navy A-7s would not drop ordnance in anger for more than eight years following the *Mayaguez* Incident, the aircraft came very close to more action just 15 months later in the wake of a seemingly innocuous event on 18 August 1976 that was dubbed the Korean Tree Incident. It would see *Midway* and CVW-5 (which included A-7A-equipped VA-56 and VA-93) sent to the Korean Peninsula.

The catalyst for this event was a seemingly innocuous plan to trim a tree that was blocking the view of a United Nations (UN) observation post in the Demilitarized Zone (DMZ) that had separated North and South Korea since the end of the Korean War in July 1953. When the Korean People's Army (KPA) ignored a request to prune the tree, US Army soldiers and Republic of Korea troops escorted civilian personnel into the treaty area on 18 August to carry out the trimming. Although not all American and South Korean servicemen were armed, selected personnel carried axes with which to carry out the pruning.

Shortly after entering the DMZ, the work party was attacked by 35 North Korean troops. Two US Army soldiers were killed, and then the KPA retreated back into North Korea – this cycle of attack and retreat was repeated for almost an hour. The KPA subsequently claimed the 'American imperialist aggressors' were at fault, and the crisis quickly escalated. US military forces in the region were ordered to DEFCON 3, indicating a heightened threat of conflict, and possibly

Armed with two Mk 84 1000-lb bombs on stations 1 and 8, A-7A BuNo 153228 of VA-93 heads for its target during a training flight from *Midway* on 21 April 1977. This aircraft had been embarked in CV-41 during the brief Operation *Paul Bunyan* deployment that had taken place eight months earlier (*US Navy*) a nuclear war. On 19 August South Korea began planning for possible rocket and artillery attacks from the North. Fortunately, no such attacks eventuated.

US forces did, however, put Operation *Paul Bunyan* (named after an American mythic folk hero lumberjack) into action on 21 August, while President Ford held a series of 'crisis talks' on how best to proceed. *Midway* was ordered to sail from its homeport of Yokosuka Naval Base, Japan, that same day, with CVW-5 embarked and its battlegroup in tow. The vessels duly headed at speed for the Korean Peninsula. It was only when the battlegroup reached the Sea of Japan the following day that flight operations began, aircraft from VA-56 and VA-93 dropping smoke markers in the water to act as targets for F-4s, A-6s and A-7s. There was planning for large-scale Alpha strikes on North Korean targets, and aircrew also began checking their personal survival gear more closely, as well as their sidearms.

By 23 August *Midway* and its battlegroup were off South Korea. Arranged on deck maintaining an Alert 5 condition were two F-4N Phantom IIs from either VF-151 or VF-161 and a pair of A-7As loaded with Mk 20 Rockeye canisters – three each on triple ejector racks (TERs) on underwing stations 1 and 8. The remaining stores stations were usually kept free of ordnance so as to reduce drag when airborne, although Corsair IIs occasionally carried the standard 300-gal fuel tanks on stations 3 and 6 so as to extend the jets' range. The A-7A's two Colt Mk 12 20 mm cannon were loaded with 340 rounds per gun.

By now, the US Army had trimmed the tree, but concern remained high about possible North Korean retaliation. The *Midway* battlegroup operated off the Korean coast until 8 September, and returned to Yokosuka eight days later

Robert Thomas, a pilot with VA-93, recalled flying an A-7A in tanker configuration from CVW-5's NAF Atsugi home to Midway shortly after the carrier departed Yokosuka on 21 August. Once off Korea, CVW-5

A-7A BuNo 153241 of VA-56 is marshalled towards *Midway*'s bow catapults during flight operations in late 1976. This aircraft, which is armed with six Mk 82 500-lb bombs on two TERs, bears the name of unit CO Cdr Robert E 'Bob' Smith beneath the cockpit. This aircraft had been one of the first A-7s to see combat in Vietnam, serving with VA-147 on board *Ranger* during the Corsair II's operational debut in 1967-68 (*US Navy*)

conducted flight operations nearly every day, as Thomas explained. 'I flew a total of 11 flights during this period, five of which were at night. We flew a longer cycle than normal, with most flights in the 2.5-hour plus range. Three of the flights – on 23, 26 and 27 August – were SUCAP [surface combat air patrol] missions. These were flown in jets with the same weaponry as the alert birds. So, in effect, we had an Alert 5 presence airborne during flight ops. We operated with VAW-115 E-2Bs and surface ships in the carrier strike group during these missions. We didn't expend any ordnance, as it was to be used operationally if required. Other flights during this period saw us undertaking practice bombing missions on mainland South Korea target ranges not far south of the DMZ, as well as carrying out routine tanker missions. One interesting tidbit is that every mission, even tanker missions, were flown with a full load of 20 mm ammunition.'

North Korean SA-2 SAM sites had their 'Spoon Rest' search radars active throughout Operation *Paul Bunyan*, but aircraft operating from *Midway* were well out of missile range. Soviet warships also routinely shadowed the battlegroup off the coast of Korea, with their fire-control radar 'painting' the US Navy vessels on occasion.

IRANIAN CRISIS

The ousting of the Shah of Iran by an anti-western Islamist regime in early 1979 saw the country go from being America's staunchest ally in the Middle East to its greatest enemy in just a few months. By the late summer, demonstrations against US interests in Iran were the order of the day, and on 4 November 1979 government-backed 'students' stormed the US Embassy in Tehran and imprisoned 66 American citizens, including 14 US Marines.

In response to the Iranian hostage crisis that commenced in November 1979, several carriers quickly made their way to the Indian Ocean to cruise for a record numbers of days. *Coral Sea* was one of these vessels, and VA-27's 'Mace 414' (BuNo 159976) was photographed taxiing in the direction of CV-43's bow catapults while carrying a 300-gal fuel tank and a single Mk 20 Rockeye on stations 7 and 8, respectively. The load on the port wing would almost certainly have been the same. The aircraft also had black-and-red identification bands on the outer starboard wing, this marking being hastily applied to a number of aircraft in CVW-14 (and CVW-8, embarked in *Nimitz*) in March 1980 (*US Navy*)

In this view of *Coral Sea*'s crowded forward flightdeck, taken on 24 March 1980, five of the seven A-7Es visible have the *Evening Light/Eagle Claw* bands encircling their starboard wingtips, as do all the F-4Ns from VMFA-323 and VMFA-531 and one of the two A-6Es from VA-196 (*US Navy*)

The catapult crew perform final safety checks on 'Mace 411' (BuNo 158834) prior to declaring the jet ready for launching from *Midway*'s solitary waist catapult on New Year's Day 1980. The aircraft is armed with six 500-lb Mk 82 Snakeye retarded bombs. The sooty deposits around the gun trough for the jet's M61 20 mm cannon denote that the weapon has been recently fired against a splash target (*US Navy*)

During the ensuing so-called hostage crisis, US Navy battlegroups that typically included an aircraft carrier would set new post-World War 2 records for the number of continuous days at sea in the Indian Ocean as they maintained a rather futile presence off the Iranian coastline for what would eventually be over a year. Beginning with *Midway*, which had arrived on station on 18 November 1979, USS *Kitty Hawk* (CV-63), USS *Nimitz* (CVN-68), *Coral Sea*, USS *Dwight D Eisenhower* (CVN-69) and USS *Independence* (CV-62), supported by various other ships of their respective battlegroups, cruised in the Indian Ocean for days on end. Each of the air wings embarked in all six carriers included two Corsair II units apiece.

The abortive rescue mission of the hostages (under the codenames Operations *Evening Light* and *Eagle Claw*) in April 1980 saw elements of both CVW-8 aboard *Nimitz* and CVW-14 aboard *Coral Sea* receive bands on their starboard wings in order to ensure visual identification against a potential enemy that also flew F-4 Phantom IIs and F-14 Tomcats. A-7Es from both ships (VA-82 and VA-86 embarked in CVN-68 and VA-27 and VA-97 on board CV-43) had black-and-red bands applied, and carried Rockeye and Mk 82 and 83 bombs. However, the much-documented tragedy of the failed rescue attempt meant that they and the other air wing assets were not required to provide force protection in the *Eagle Claw* extraction phase. With the release of the hostages in January 1981 following Ronald Reagan's presidential victory two months earlier, the crisis abated and the international atmosphere quieted down for a while.

Between November 1979 and July 1980, the six carriers had steamed for 529 days in the Indian Ocean and Arabian Gulf. *Dwight D Eisenhower* (with CVW-7, including VA-12 and VA-66, embarked) had relieved *Nimitz* on 29 April 1980, and by the time CVN-69 returned to its homeport of Norfolk, Virginia, on 22 December, the carrier and its battlegroup had been deployed for a record 251 days – 'Ike' was underway at sea for 153 continuous days.

The Middle East would become an increasingly familiar region to US carrier-borne forces.

CHAPTER THREE

THE TURBULENT 1980s

Lebanon had become a refuge for a number of factions that were anti-Israeli and which, in turn, attracted the support of neighbouring Syria. With both the USA and the Soviet Union standing behind Israel and Syria, respectively, the early 1980s saw the Lebanese government paralysed as its country began a rapid descent into conflict. As a result, the Regan Administration's policy determined that US naval forces took the lead in protecting American nationals in the country, starting with contingency operations in the eastern Mediterranean in the spring/summer of 1981 by USS *Forrestal* (CV-59) and its embarked air wing, CVW-17 (which included VA-81 and VA-83).

And so began something of a shuttle service as carrier battlegroups moved back and forth from the Mediterranean to the Indian Ocean and back again as the international situation required an American presence off the Lebanese coast as well as the Arabian Gulf region.

When the Lebanese government collapsed on 24 June 1982, Israel invaded its neighbour. *Dwight D Eisenhower*, embarking CVW-7, was already sailing on the modified location nicknamed Bagel Station (the name's derivation is unsure but could relate to its proximity to Israel) to the south of Cyprus as a contingency to oversee the rescue of US nationals in Lebanon. In the following months, US carrier coverage off the Lebanese coast was almost without interval, not only for protecting Marines that had deployed ashore as part of a multinational peacekeeping

A four-ship of A-7Es from VA-66 closes up for the benefit of the camera during a training mission just prior to joining *Dwight D Eisenhower* for its 1980 Mediterranean/ Indian Ocean deployment. 'Ike', with CVW-7 embarked, was on cruise from 15 April to 22 December 1980. BuNo 158669, in the foreground, would serve with VA-66 from 1975 through to 1982 (*US Navy*)

Looking pristine, bar the soot deposits forward of the 20 mm cannon muzzle, VA-81's 'CAG bird' is prepared for a tanker mission from *Saratoga* during the carrier's 1983 Mediterranean deployment. Befitting its role as the A-7 assigned to the air wing commander, the Corsair II has coloured chevrons on its rudder (*US Navy*)

CVN-69 completes an underway replenishment from USS *Savannah* (AOR-4) while conducting 'contingency ops' on Bagel Station off the coast of Lebanon in August 1983. Amongst the aircraft from CVW-7 chained down on its flightdeck are Corsair IIs of VA-12 and VA-66 (*US Navy*)

force, but also as the US National Command Authority did not wish to allow Syria (and its Soviet puppet masters) a greater stance in the region. *Eisenhower*, now conducting its 1983 cruise, was back on Bagel Station on 7 June that year, undertaking 'contingency ops' that saw the Corsair IIs of VA-12 and VA-66 holding deck alert postures alongside limited flight operations.

In September, both units flew daily patrols off Lebanon supporting the peacekeepers of the Multinational Force, armed and ready to answer a call to support US Navy warships that were occasionally coming under fire from Syrian rebel positions fighting the established government in Lebanon. It was a very involved and often confusing situation that would soon come to a much-needed defining point where the US Navy carriers would have to be called into action.

GRENADA

Lebanon remained the focal point for the White House. On 23 October 1983, the driver of a truck packed with explosives rammed the vehicle into the US Marine Corps barracks at Beirut International Airport. The subsequent blast killed 241 service personnel, mostly Marines. Three days later, *Eisenhower* sailed from Naples, Italy, to the eastern Mediterranean, where it was later joined by USS *John F Kennedy* (CV-67) and *Independence*.

CV-62 had departed Norfolk on 18 October 1983, with both the ship and CVW-6 (including VA-15 and VA-87) expecting to proceed directly to the Mediterranean to relieve *Eisenhower* on

Bagel Station. However, instead of heading east across the Atlantic, the carrier and its battlegroup sailed south. Their new destination, which had been a closely kept secret, was the small southeastern Caribbean island of Grenada, situated 80 miles north of Venezuela. The Reagan Administration had determined that the country's New Jewel Movement government (which had seized power on 19 October 1983) had moved too far towards the communist sphere, stating that its close relationship with Cuba was particularly worrisome. There was also concern that expansion at the island's primary airport would facilitate its use by Soviet long-range bombers.

These two A-7Es from VA-66 (BuNo 157541 in the foreground and BuNo 160736) clearly show how US Navy camouflage changed in the early 1980s with the fleet-wide adoption of the Tactical Paint Scheme (TPS). The pilots of these jets – both of which are carrying AN/AAR-45 FLIR pods and empty practice bomb racks – were undertaking an aerial refuelling qualification sortie during 'Ike's' 1983 deployment when they were photographed by Lt Stu Davis, who was flying a 'KA-7E' tanker (*US Navy*)

On the day of the catastrophic bombing of the Marine barracks in Beirut, Cdr Michael O'Brien, CO of VA-87 aboard 'Indy', received word that the carrier was detouring from its course for Lebanon to Grenada to protect American citizens as part of Operation *Urgent Fury*. The nine squadrons of CVW-6 prepared for this surprising turn of events, with the two A-7 units and VA-176 (the air wing's sole A-6 squadron) in the thick of the action. The operation required dividing the island in half, with the US Navy and US Marine Corps taking the northern half and the US Army and USAF being responsible for the southern half.

At 0500 hrs on 25 October, 400 Marines from the 22nd Marine Amphibious Unit embarked in the amphibious assault ship USS *Guam* (LPH-9) boarded CH-46 helicopters. They landed at Pearls Airport without meeting any enemy resistance. At about the same time, Army Rangers and members of the 82nd Airborne Division parachuted from USAF transports onto Point Salines Airport on the southern tip of Grenada. Unlike the Marines, the Rangers encountered fairly strong opposition from more than 100 Cuban and Grenadian soldiers. They duly called for help, and 'Indy's' A-7s went in.

The pilot of VA-87's 'CAG bird', 'War Party 400' (BuNo 160560), demonstrates a shallow dive delivery profile with four Mk 83 1000-lb bombs during the early weeks of the unit's highly eventful 1983-84 deployment with CVW-6 embarked in *Independence* (*US Navy*)

Cdr O'Brien led a division of four VA-87 A-7Es, with their target being Richmond Hill prison at Fort Frederick, north of Point Salines Airport and east of St Georges. The aircraft destroyed several buildings and key defensive sites with Mk 82 500-lb bombs, Rockeyes and strafing runs. The A-7s' close air support (CAS) enabled US troops to seize Soviet and Cuban weapons and

VA-87's 'War Party 406' (BuNo 160554) circles Point Salines Airport on the southern tip of Grenada. This was the site of some of the bloodiest fighting of *Urgent Fury* due to the runway being defended by more than 100 Cuban and Grenadian soldiers. VA-87 played a key role in helping US Army Rangers seize the airport, flying a number of CAS missions that saw Mk 82 500-lb bombs and Rockeye and APAM canisters dropped, followed by multiple strafing runs. This aircraft is carrying both an APAM canister and a Mk 82 bomb, along with a 300-gal tank, on stations 6, 7 and 8 (*US Navy*)

equipment, as well as allowing the Rangers to capture enemy defences around Point Salines Airport.

Following this action, both A-7 squadrons were called on to strafe enemy gun sites at St Georges Bay after the loss of two US Marine Corps AH-1 Sea Cobra gunships – three of the four pilots involved were killed and the one survivor seriously injured. As these guns were not radar-directed, and were thus less effective against fast jets, they were able to hit the helicopters flying at 100 knots.

The following day, Cdr O'Brien launched with a second A-7 flown by Lt D M Nehilla to support US Army infantry pinned down by heavy automatic weapons fire from Cuban and Grenadian soldiers. Marine Capt Pieter M Velzeboer, a forward observer attached to the US Army, coordinated the A-7s' strafing passes. He later wrote, in part, the Corsair IIs 'came out of nowhere and strafed the target. They directly caused the Cuban garrison to surrender, and made a difficult job quite easy'. Cdr O'Brien added, 'We would send up several A-7s [from both VA-15 and VA-87] and some A-6s from VA-176. After the third day, they helped flush out some small remaining pockets of Cubans who had fled into the hills'.

On 27 October, both squadrons attacked the Calivigny military barracks on Grenada's southeastern coast. This mission was a good example of how the two 'Indy' Corsair II squadrons worked together, with four A-7s from each unit hitting the barracks. The latter was actually a terrorist and guerilla training camp that the Cubans had used in a last ditch stand to defend against advancing American troops. The US Navy jets levelled many of the barracks' buildings with bombs and Cluster Bomb Units (CBUs), with pilots also expending more than 7000 rounds of 20 mm ammunition. It proved to be the last serious attack mission of *Urgent Fury*.

Although VA-176's Intruders saw action in Grenada, it was the A-7s from VA-15 and VA-87 that undertook the bulk of the missions for CVW-6 – possibly because of the Corsair II's proven strafing capabilities. Although the aircraft's 20 mm cannon proved a great success in *Urgent Fury*, communication between A-7 pilots and US Army troops on the ground proved more problematic. Indeed, these issues were highlighted by Secretary of the Navy John Lehman in his book *Command of the Seas*. While the problem was prevalent throughout the campaign, it became more evident in the actions directly involving the two Corsair II squadrons because each party did not have exactly the same communications gear and setups. Although the A-7s carried UHF radios for working with the US Marine Corps and other US Navy compatriots, they lacked the VHF equipment US Army troops were using in the southern half of Grenada, where most of the action occurred. Somehow, the calls and tasking got through and the Naval Aviators did their job, much to their credit.

Another hurdle overcome by the A-7 units was the limited choice of ordnance on board CV-62. Although the carrier had iron bombs in the

form of Mk 82 '500 pounders', new CBU-59 'Anti-Personnel/Anti-Material' (APAM) bomblet containers similar to the earlier Mk 20 Rockeye and ammunition for the A-7E's single internal 20 mm cannon, it lacked rockets such as the much-used Zuni 5-inch or 2.75-inch weapons. With strafing proving so popular in *Urgent Fury*, and other aircraft in CVW-6 lacking this capability (the F-14As from VF-14 and VF-32 also had internal 20 mm cannon but their crews were not well-versed in CAS, and the A-6s lacked a gun), the A-7s were for all intents and purposes the only true CAS assets available. The jet's importance in the Grenada operation was summed up in VA-87's Command History Report for 1983 as follows;

'The Corsair II's timely response was credited with shortening the conflict and saving American lives. In the words of Vice Admiral Joseph Metcalf [Operational Commander of all US forces involved in *Urgent Fury*], "the A-7 provided the turning point in the battle for St George, allowing the multinational force [from Jamaica, Barbados, Venezuela and the US] to quickly gain the upper hand". Vice Admiral Metcalf had only the highest praise for the pinpoint accuracy of the A-7's bombs and bullets.'

VA-15's Command History Report for 1983 noted that the unit was involved in combat operations over Grenada for eight days from 25 October, during which time its pilots flew more than 140 CAS missions delivering 21 Mk 20 Rockeye canisters and 21 Mk 82 low-drag general-purpose (LDGP) bombs and expending 18,700 20 mm cannon rounds.

For the light attack pilots supporting ground troops, Grenada provided an uncommonly permissive environment. There were no enemy radars to jam or deceive and no SAMs to evade. The A-7 pilots could assemble over a pre-selected anchor point, pick up contact with a FAC, proceed to the target at almost any altitude unless ZSU-23-2 23 mm AAA fire was encountered, and make their run-ins without any significant concerns.

After final mopping-up activities, *Independence* and its battlegroup resumed their interrupted journey toward Lebanon, where more action was waiting a month later.

'War Party 401' (BuNo 156807 – the oldest Corsair II assigned to either unit in CVW-6 in 1983) heads for a target in southern Grenada armed with a CBU-59 APAM canister. There was probably another canister on the starboard side. Note the black lightning bolt on the APAM indicating that it was the more advanced Rockeye variant. The original Mk 20 Rockeye contained 247 bomblets with small warheads for use against trucks, artillery and semi-hardened targets, while the newer CBU-59 APAM contained 650 bomblets, smaller still but more grenade-like. They could discriminate between soft and hard targets. If there were no hard targets, the APAM bomblet would spring into the air and act like a grenade (*US Navy*)

CHAPTER FOUR

MORE ACTION IN THE MIDDLE EAST

A-7s from VA-15 and VA-87 are chained down over bow catapult two on board *Independence* in early December 1983, shortly before CTF-60's disastrous Alpha strike against Syrian-manned positions in Lebanon. All of the jets appear to be carrying AN/AAR-45 FLIR pods and either Mk 20 Rockeye or CBU-59 APAM canisters (*US Navy*)

Cdr Edward K Andrews had assumed command of CVW-6 aboard *Independence* on 1 November 1982, with the air wing and its carrier nearing the end of a routine six-month-long Mediterranean deployment. He was a colourful, highly experienced Naval Aviator with the improbable call sign of 'Hunyak', whose meaning can be taken as impetuous, wild or stubborn, among other definitions. A native of Macomb, Illinois, Andrews had flown RF-8G Crusaders with VFP-62 over Vietnam from USS *Franklin D. Roosevelt* (CVA-42) during the carrier's and squadron's only combat deployment. He had subsequently switched to F-14s, serving with VF-32 and VF-84 (he was CO of the latter squadron) prior to taking command of CVW-6. As part of assuming the CAG (Carrier Air Wing commander) role, Andrews was new to the A-7, and he would see his first combat in the aircraft with CVW-6 when he flew a few missions in Grenada.

As *Independence* and its air wing headed across the Atlantic towards the Mediterranean in early November 1983, the ship and CVW-6 took stock. Operation *Urgent Fury* had provided a useful tune-up for a new deployment, the carrier duly relieving 'Ike' and CVW-7 and coming under

Sixth Fleet control. CV-62 joined *John F Kennedy* and CVW-3 in the eastern Mediterranean, CV-67 and its 'all-Grumman' air wing – so called because it included two larger VA(Medium) A-6-equipped units and no A-7 light attack assets – having been operating off Lebanon for several weeks already.

Daily, US and French carriers sent aircraft on patrol and reconnaissance missions to provide intelligence to UN peacekeeping commanders on the ground in Lebanon. Tactical Airborne Reconnaissance Pod System (TARPS)-equipped F-14As were a key asset in performing this role, the aircraft overflying Lebanon taking photographs of the positions occupied by Syrian, Druze militia and pro-Syrian Palestinian guerilla forces. On 3 December two Tomcats from VF-31 launched from 'JFK' to conduct just such a mission. The TARPS jets usually met some form of light flak as they sped across their target area at 600 knots and 3500 ft. On that day, however, the VF-31 crews spotted several tell-tale corkscrew smoke trails of SA-7 shoulder-launched SAMs.

The militia and their Syrian backers had upped the ante, prompting the Reagan Administration to consider an appropriate response. President Reagan finally ordered an air strike akin to a Vietnam-era Alpha Strike, involving aircraft from both carriers armed with heavy ordnance for employment against one important target. It was something that many of the senior personnel in the air wing knew well. Both CVW-3 and CVW-6 had developed target sets prior to reaching Bagel Station, and these had been regularly updated following the daily TARPS runs.

Embarked in CV-67 was the Commander of Carrier Group Two, and dual-hatted as Commander, Task Force 60 (CTF-60), Rear Admiral Jerry O Tuttle, himself a former A-7 pilot and a very strong, demanding individual who did not countenance lackadaisical planning or execution. Tuttle had flown A-4Cs with VA-15 from USS *Intrepid* (CVS-11) in 1967,

Independence underway off Lebanon in December 1983. The carrier's forward flightdeck is crowded with aircraft from CVW-6 as flight operations are about to resume. CV-62 spent the majority of its time on Bagel Station during the carrier's 1983-84 deployment, which lasted six months (*US Navy*)

logging 260 missions, 220 of them over North Vietnam. He had also commanded A-7E-equipped VA-81 in 1972 and had been the CO of 'JFK' in 1976-78. Tuttle was thus a highly experienced and heavily decorated combat aviator who knew well one of the carriers he was about to send into battle.

According to one of Tuttle's staff officers, Lt Cdr Joe Hulsey, 'We had been on constant alert for weeks, with one carrier being in "alert 30" with aircraft fully loaded and crews briefed, while the other flightdeck conducted normal flight ops. This changed every 24 hours in order to share the load. The force was ready, having prepared more than 300 potential targets in the region. We had timing and weapons loads planned for all of them, and all of this information was sent up the chain to Sixth Fleet and CINCUSNAVFOREUR [Commander-in-Chief, US Naval Forces Europe] so that they'd know what we were prepared to do. On top of that, we had Jerry Tuttle in charge. He was exactly who you'd want in that position if you were going over the beach'.

The hair-trigger conditions continued through to 1 December, when the carriers received direction to stand down from constant alert. Then, at about 0300 hrs on the morning of the 3rd, a Flash order arrived from Sixth Fleet to execute strikes against six specific targets (four for CVW-3 and two for CVW-6) in Lebanon, with a time on target (ToT) of only four hours later. The order was initially believed by the staff to have been sent in error, but as messages and voice traffic flashed between the ships and Sixth Fleet it became obvious that 'somebody' much higher had decided on military action with absolutely no regard for what it took for the operational forces to actually execute it.

Ordnance personnel attach Mk 20 Rockeye canisters to a TER that will then be winched up and locked onto station 8 of an A-7 on board 'Indy' in early December 1983. A fully loaded TER has already been bolted into place on station 7 (*US Navy*)

VA-15's 'Active Boy 314' (BuNo 159971) launches from 'Indy's' bow catapult one at the start of a training mission in November 1983. The aircraft is 'armed' with blue inert Mk 82 bombs on a TER attached to station 1 (*US Navy*)

Aircraft were not ready or correctly spotted on either flightdeck, proper ordnance was not loaded and crews were not briefed. On top of that, only one of the six specified targets had actually been prepared by the ships, and the other five, considered militarily irrelevant, were all new. While the carriers rapidly woke up, it was confirmed that the ToT was an absolute that had to be met, which led to an all-hands effort to carry out the orders.

Unlike CAG Andrews of CVW-6, CVW-3's Cdr John J Mazach was a former Corsair II pilot, with combat time flying A-7Bs with VA-87 from USS *Ticonderoga* (CVA-14) in 1969 during the B-model's first operational deployment. This time, however, Mazach (who would eventually rise to the rank of vice admiral) would lead his air wing from the cockpit of a VA-85 A-6, while Andrews would participate in the strike at the controls of an A-7 from VA-15.

John F Kennedy launched 12 Intruders (seven from VA-85 and five from VA-75) and *Independence* sent five aloft, along with several KA-6Ds. Six A-7Es – armed with a mix of Mk 20 Rockeye and APAM canisters and 1000 rounds of 20mm ammunition – from 'Indy' went as well, as did Tomcats and Prowlers from both carriers. Ordnance loads were limited by the time available and, in most cases, not optimum for their targets – a battlefield surveillance radar, Syrian tanks and three artillery sites (which had 28 gun emplacements between them) in Lebanon's Bekaa Valley, close to the Syrian border. Only one Intruder from CV-67 got off with a full bomb load. Aircraft went feet dry at medium altitude at dawn, and almost immediately were engulfed by AAA and missiles. While EA-6Bs appeared to render any radar-guided SAMs ineffective, the sky was full of infrared-guided weapons blind to the Prowlers' magic.

The aircraft were opposed by an intimidating array of SAMs that the Soviets had supplied to their Syrian allies, who had in turn passed them on to the Lebanese factions they supported. These weapons included SA-5 and

SA-6 medium-to-high altitude SAMs and short-range shoulder-launched SA-7s, as well as derivative SA-8 and SA-9 variants of the latter missile. There were also plenty of highly mobile, radar-directed, ZSU-23-4 23mm flak batteries surrounding Beirut too, these weapons having proven very effective against low-flying aircraft in Vietnam.

With the change in ToT and the target list determined in Washington, D.C. differing significantly from those familiar to the air wings, the entire launch sequence was terribly confused. Sleeping crews had to be awakened, pulled from their bunks to attend earlier-than-planned briefings and conduct pre-flight checks on their assigned aircraft on the carriers' darkened flightdecks. Many Intruder crews would be unhappy to find their aircraft poorly armed, with several A-6s only carrying a few APAM or Rockeye canisters. The red-shirted ordnance men had not had the time or the appropriate number of stores to fully load their aircraft. This problem did not affect the A-7 units, however.

As fate would have it, the only fully loaded Intruder (from VA-85) would be the one A-6 to be shot down when it was hit by a SAM (probably an SA-7) as the jet neared the target. Its crew ejected with injuries that would see the pilot die on the ground and the bombardier/navigator spend nearly a month in captivity before diplomatic efforts got him released and repatriated.

'Indy's' A-6s and A-7s were tasked with attacking a Syrian-operated Stentor battlefield surveillance radar and elements of the Syrian Army's 27th Artillery Brigade dug in near the village of Hammana. Both targets had supposedly been chosen in Washington, D.C. because of the threat they posed to Marines based in and around Beirut International Airport, and due to the fact that they could be hit with a minimum potential of collateral damage and casualties amongst the civilian population.

The six A-7s would be led aloft by VA-15 CO Cdr Byron Duff, with CAG Andrews as his 'dash two'. Duff and Andrews would target the Stentor radar, while his XO, Cdr Leslie Kappel, led four A-7s in the strike on the artillery site near Hammana. Cdr Duff later reported that CAG Andrews had visited every squadron ready room to encourage the men of his air wing about to launch on what for many of them would be their first combat mission. Once on the flightdeck, he made it a point to visit each aircraft to talk with its pilot or aircrew.

On 'Indy's' flightdeck, the A-7s of the two squadrons made their way to their catapults. CAG Andrews was still new to the Corsair II, with its suite of advanced avionics that made the jet such a successful attack platform. His aircraft, AE 305 (BuNo 157468),

VA-87's 'War Party 404' (BuNo 156862), armed with Mk 20 Rockeye, taxies towards 'Indy's' bow catapults on the day of the strike against Syrian-manned battlefield surveillance radar and artillery sites. The aircraft is also carrying an AIM-9L for self-protection in the event Syrian Arab Air Force fighters try to interfere with the attack (*US Navy*)

was lightly armed with only six CBU-59 APAM canisters, three each on a TER on the outermost underwing stations, numbers 1 and 8, along with a 300-gal fuel tank on station 3, close to the port side of the fuselage, and a single AIM-9 Sidewinder on the cheek station 4 on the fuselage's port side, just in case. No Sidewinder was carried on the starboard cheek station 5 because station 6 carried a forward-looking infrared (FLIR) sensor mounted in an AN/AAR-45 pod. No other stores stations were wired to carry the latter, and there were concerns the missile's ignition flame might fry the sensitive FLIR.

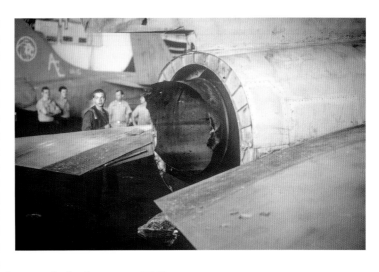

VA-15's 'Active Boy 314' (BuNo 159971), flown by unit XO Cdr Leslie Kappel, was hit in the tail by a shoulder-launched SA-7 SAM while leading the attack on the guns of the 27th Artillery Brigade dug in near the village of Hammana. The pilot made it back to 'Indy' and successfully recovered aboard the carrier, with one Mk 20 Rockeye canister still attached to station 7. The jet was quickly repaired and returned to service with VA-15 (*US Navy*)

As the A-7s began launching, Andrews had problems. His jet's avionics were 'dead'. He had not pushed their circuit breakers during his pre-flight walk-around – a neophyte's mistake, and fortunately easily corrected. The second problem was a little more serious. As the flightdeck crew brought him out of his position to taxi toward the catapult, the Corsair II's nose gear steering failed. Ordinarily, the jet would have been downed, and scrubbed from the launch cycle. But even though the yellow-shirted flight director was indicating that his aircraft would not fly, CAG shook his head vigorously. There was absolutely no way he was not going to make this flight. If Andrews launched he could fly the mission and deliver his ordnance, but recovery back aboard was problematic. The enlisted squadron maintenance chief petty officer scampered up onto the side of the fuselage of the now-lame A-7 with the frustrated air wing commander strapped into the jet's ejection seat.

Up in 'Indy's' Pri-fly, the bay-windowed 'tower' that overlooked the flightdeck, the Air Boss, Capt George Lundy Jr, was watching the proceedings aft of the starboard bow catapult. He called to see what the delay was. When he learned the pilot in the stuck A-7 was his friend CAG Andrews, he knew there was only one way to go. He and 'Hunyak' had been shipmates aboard CV-67 when Andrews was flying F-14s with VF-32 and Lundy was an A-7 pilot with VA-46.

From his position over the flightdeck, Lundy could see that CAG's Corsair II was not yet on the catapult, slowing the launch sequence. Something had to be done, and quickly. He told the deck crew to launch the CAG. They would worry about the stuck nose gear and the recovery later. It was a bold decision that in the event would not have to be revisited. Cdr Andrews was finally in the air with his air wing, where he belonged, flying on the wing of Cdr Byron Duff.

All aircraft launched under the handicap of early morning darkness and the fact they would be heading into the sun over their targets. When they arrived, they were met with increasing enemy defensive fire, AAA and SAMs. The strike led by Cdr Kappel (four A-7s and five A-6s) found its target – the guns of the 27th Artillery Brigade. (*text continues on page 48*)

COLOUR PLATES

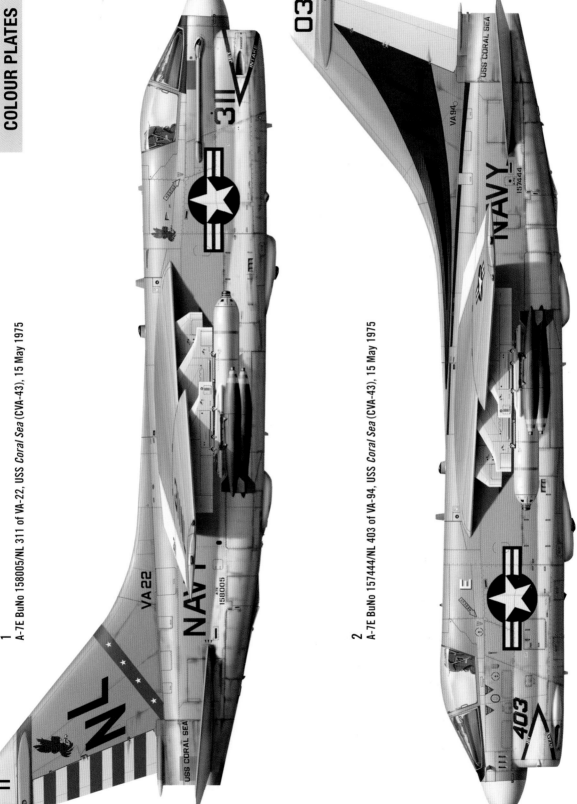

1
A-7E BuNo 158005/NL 311 of VA-22, USS *Coral Sea* (CVA-43), 15 May 1975

2
A-7E BuNo 157444/NL 403 of VA-94, USS *Coral Sea* (CVA-43), 15 May 1975

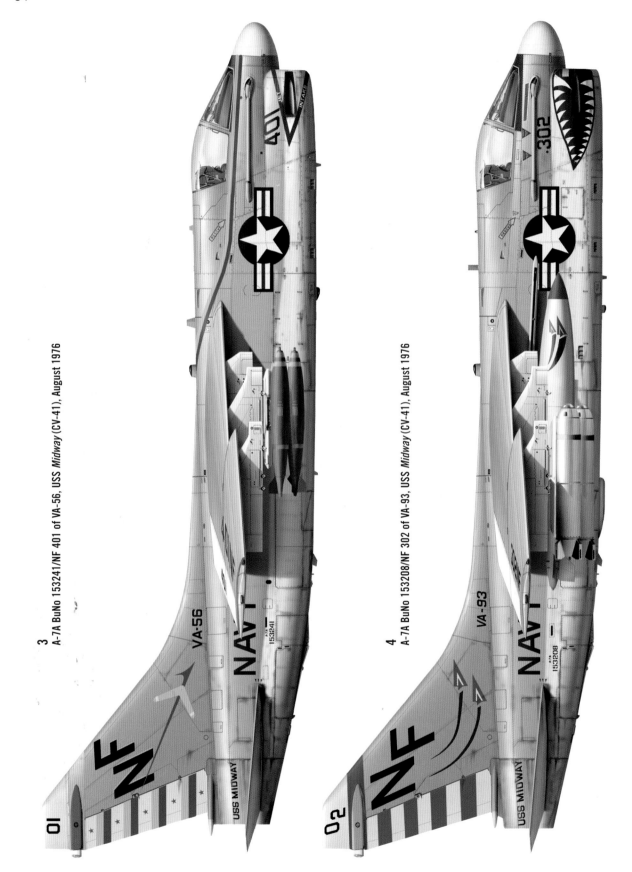

3
A-7A BuNo 153241/NF 401 of VA-56, USS *Midway* (CV-41), August 1976

4
A-7A BuNo 153208/NF 302 of VA-93, USS *Midway* (CV-41), August 1976

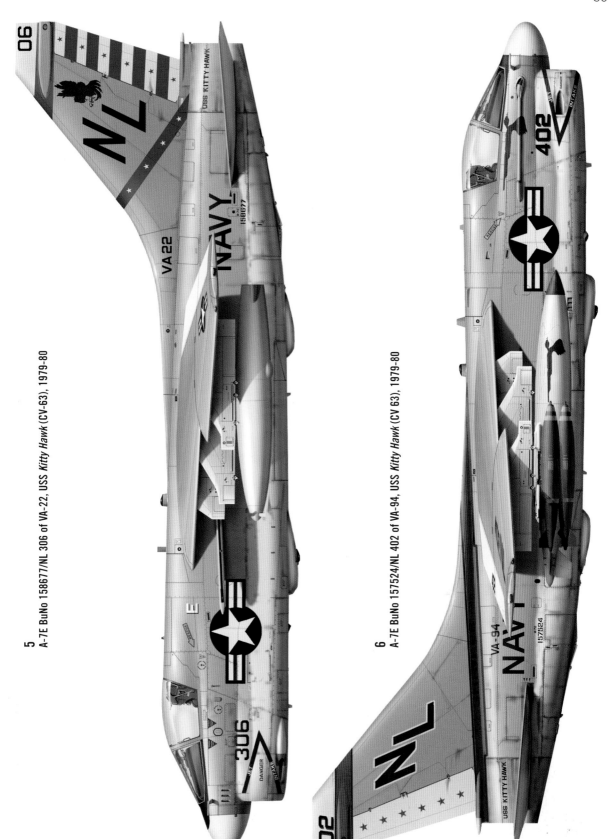

5
A-7E BuNo 158677/NL 306 of VA-22, USS *Kitty Hawk* (CV-63), 1979–80

6
A-7E BuNo 157524/NL 402 of VA-94, USS *Kitty Hawk* (CV 63), 1979–80

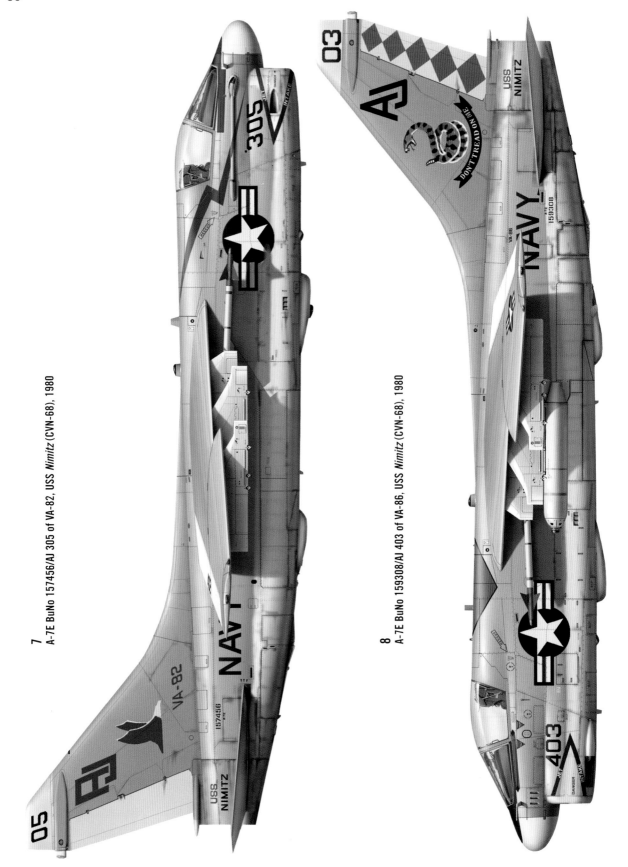

7
A-7E BuNo 157456/AJ 305 of VA-82, USS *Nimitz* (CVN-68), 1980

8
A-7E BuNo 159308/AJ 403 of VA-86, USS *Nimitz* (CVN-68), 1980

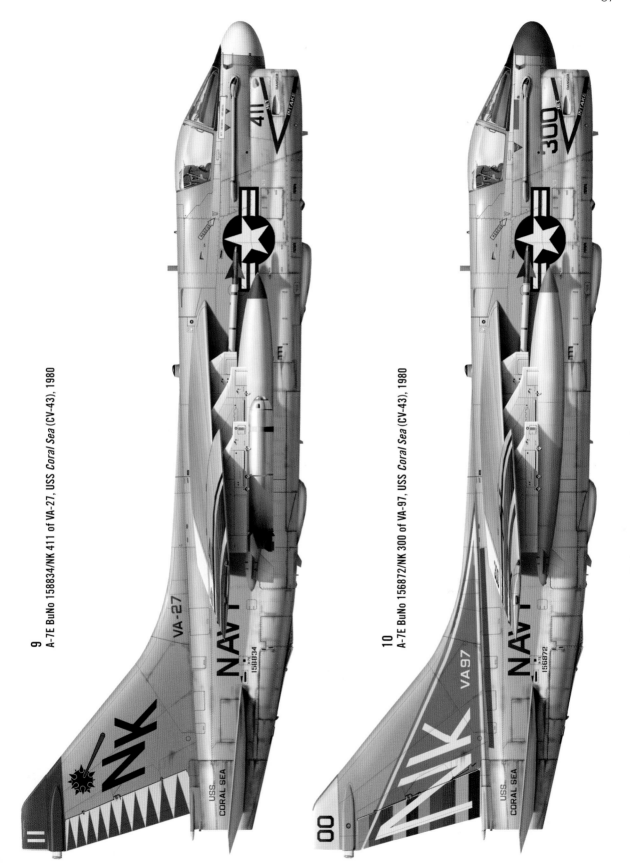

9
A-7E BuNo 158834/NK 411 of VA-27, USS *Coral Sea* (CV-43), 1980

10
A-7E BuNo 156872/NK 300 of VA-97, USS *Coral Sea* (CV-43), 1980

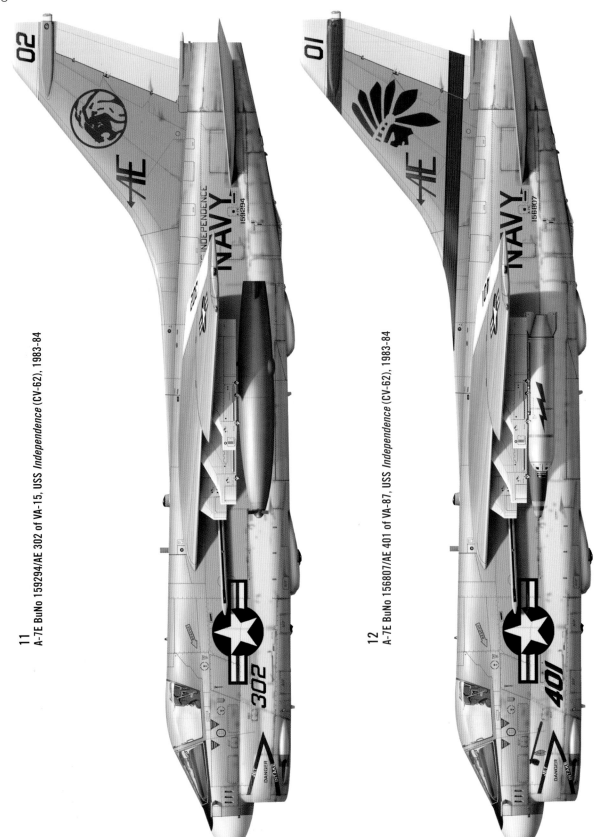

11
A-7E BuNo 159294/AE 302 of VA-15, USS *Independence* (CV-62), 1983-84

12
A-7E BuNo 156807/AE 401 of VA-87, USS *Independence* (CV-62), 1983-84

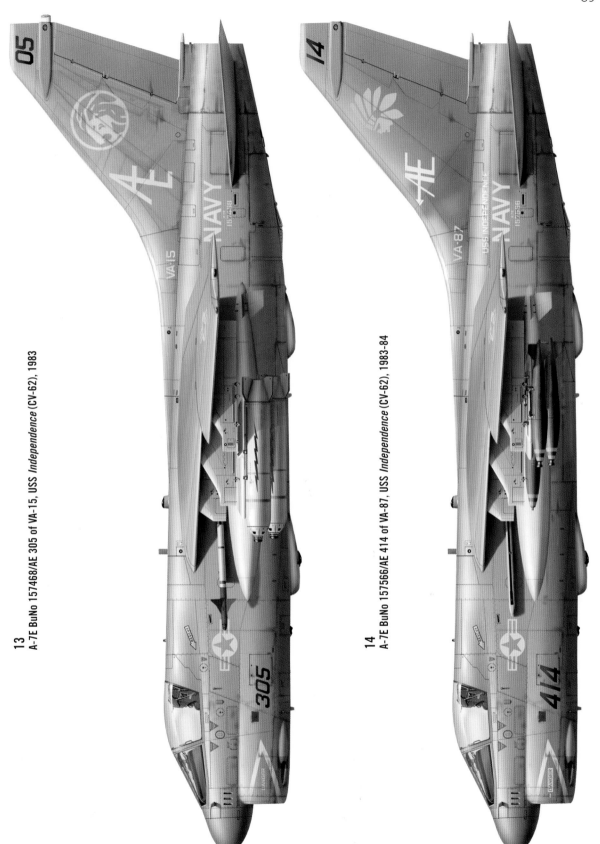

13
A-7E BuNo 157468/AE 305 of VA-15, USS *Independence* (CV-62), 1983

14
A-7E BuNo 157566/AE 414 of VA-87, USS *Independence* (CV-62), 1983-84

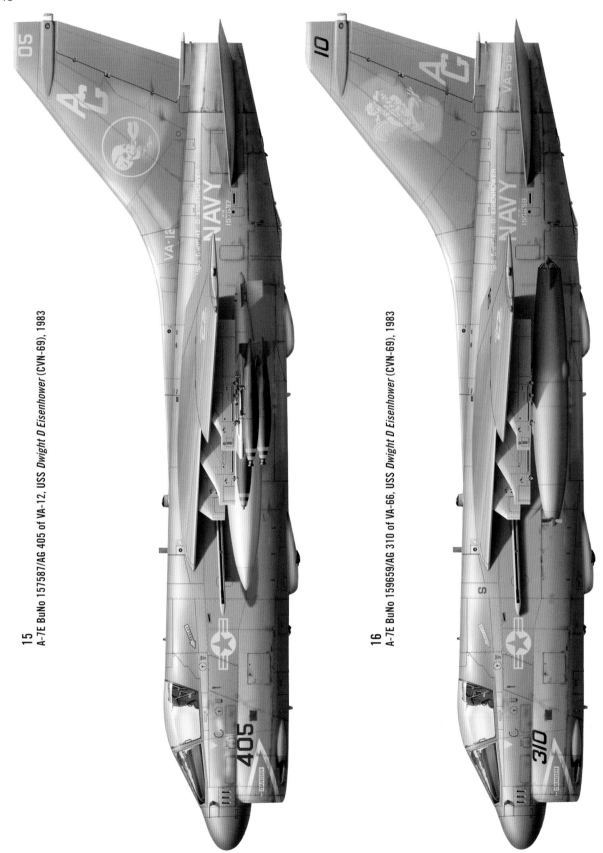

15
A-7E BuNo 157587/AG 405 of VA-12, USS *Dwight D Eisenhower* (CVN-69), 1983

16
A-7E BuNo 159659/AG 310 of VA-66, USS *Dwight D Eisenhower* (CVN-69), 1983

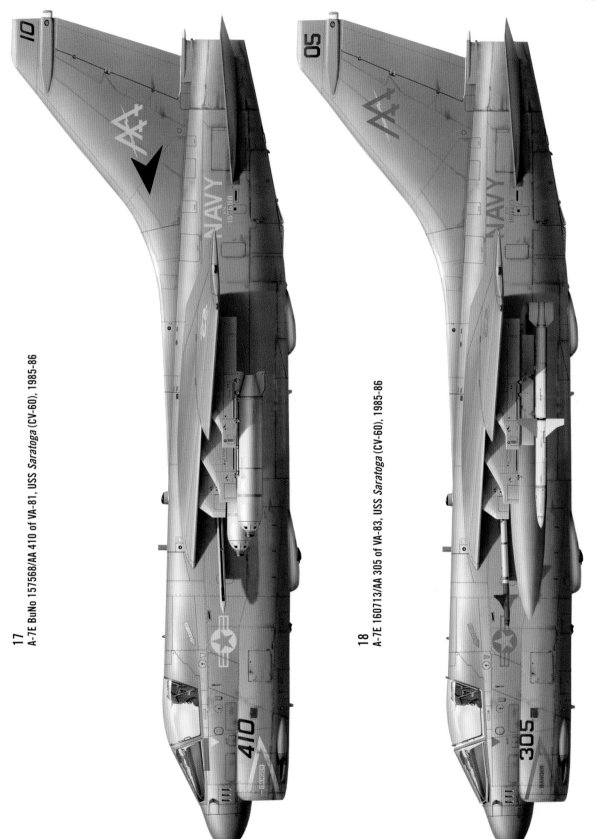

17
A-7E BuNo 157568/AA 410 of VA-81, USS *Saratoga* (CV-60), 1985-86

18
A-7E 160713/AA 305 of VA-83, USS *Saratoga* (CV-60), 1985-86

42

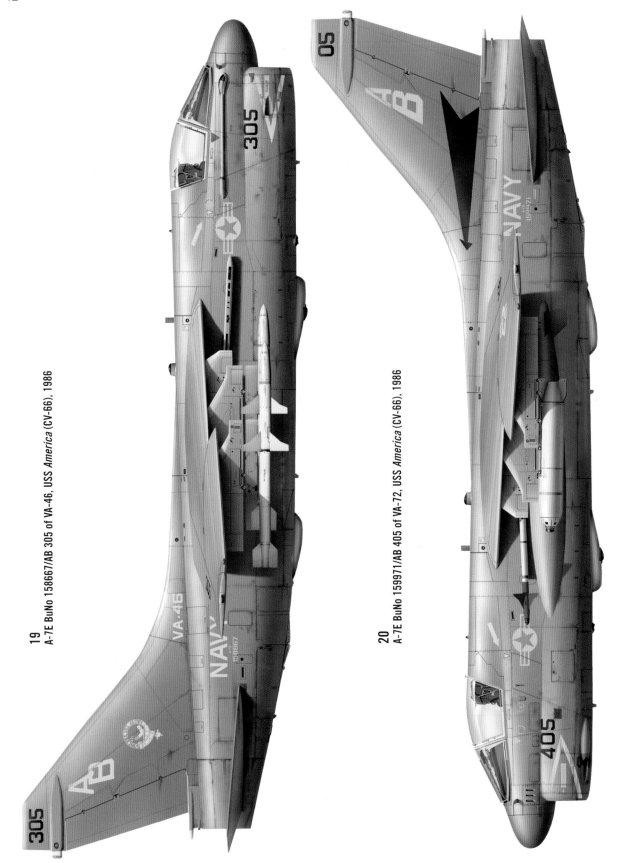

19
A-7E BuNo 158667/AB 305 of VA-46, USS *America* (CV-66), 1986

20
A-7E BuNo 159971/AB 405 of VA-72, USS *America* (CV-66), 1986

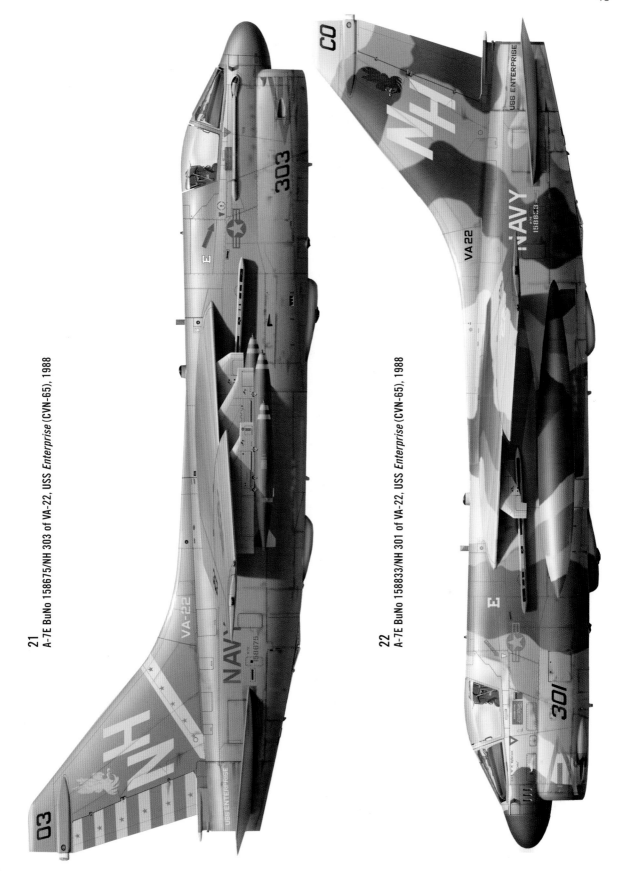

21
A-7E BuNo 158675/NH 303 of VA-22, USS *Enterprise* (CVN-65), 1988

22
A-7E BuNo 158833/NH 301 of VA-22, USS *Enterprise* (CVN-65), 1988

44

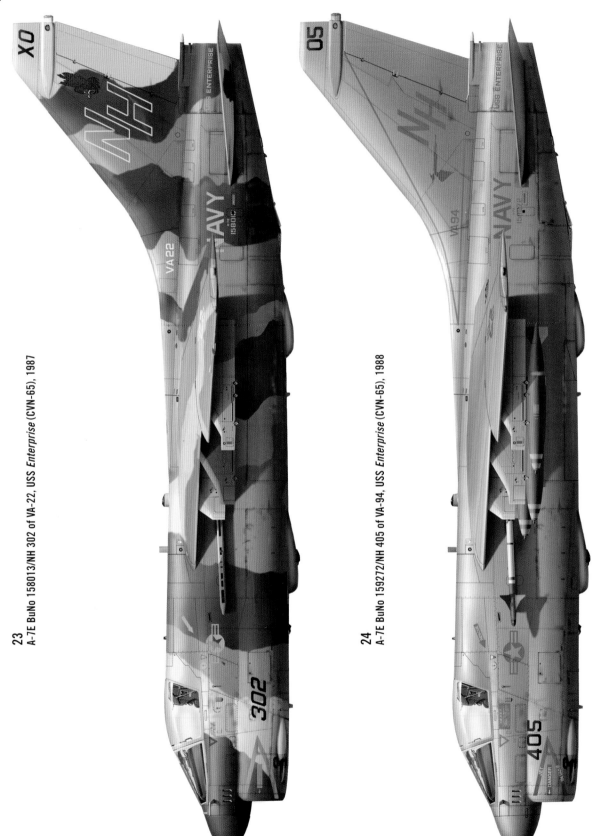

23
A-7E BuNo 158013/NH 302 of VA-22, USS *Enterprise* (CVN-65), 1987

24
A-7E BuNo 159272/NH 405 of VA-94, USS *Enterprise* (CVN-65), 1988

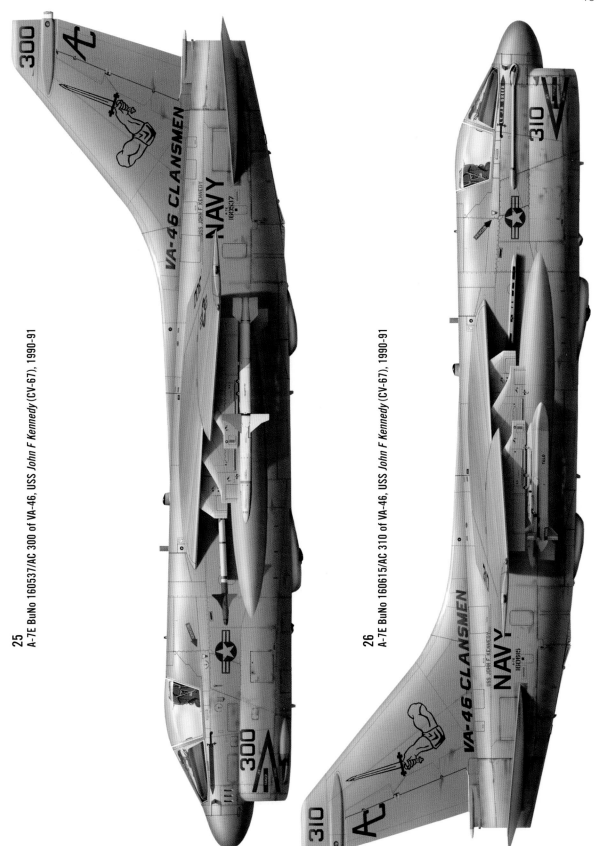

25
A-7E BuNo 160537/AC 300 of VA-46, USS *John F Kennedy* (CV-67), 1990–91

26
A-7E BuNo 160615/AC 310 of VA-46, USS *John F Kennedy* (CV-67), 1990–91

46

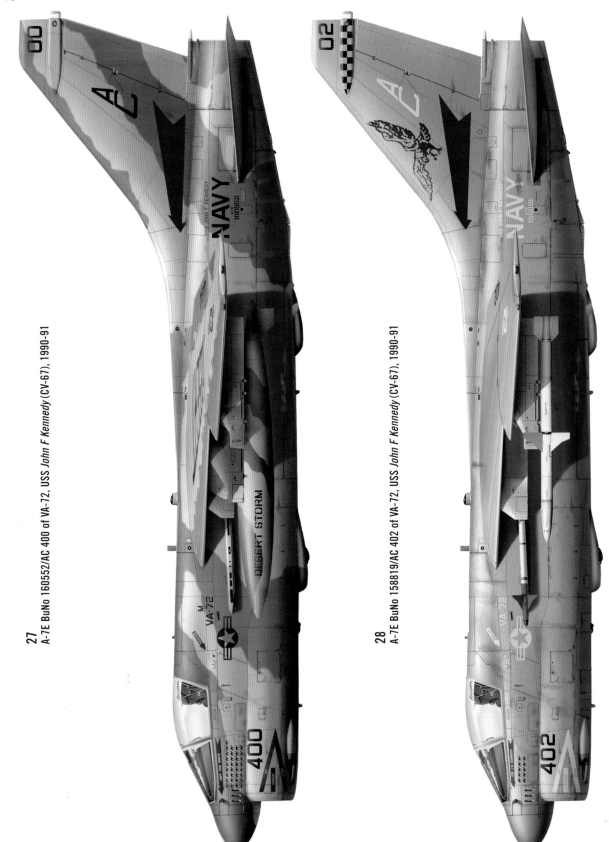

27
A-7E BuNo 160552/AC 400 of VA-72, USS *John F Kennedy* (CV-67), 1990-91

28
A-7E BuNo 158819/AC 402 of VA-72, USS *John F Kennedy* (CV-67), 1990-91

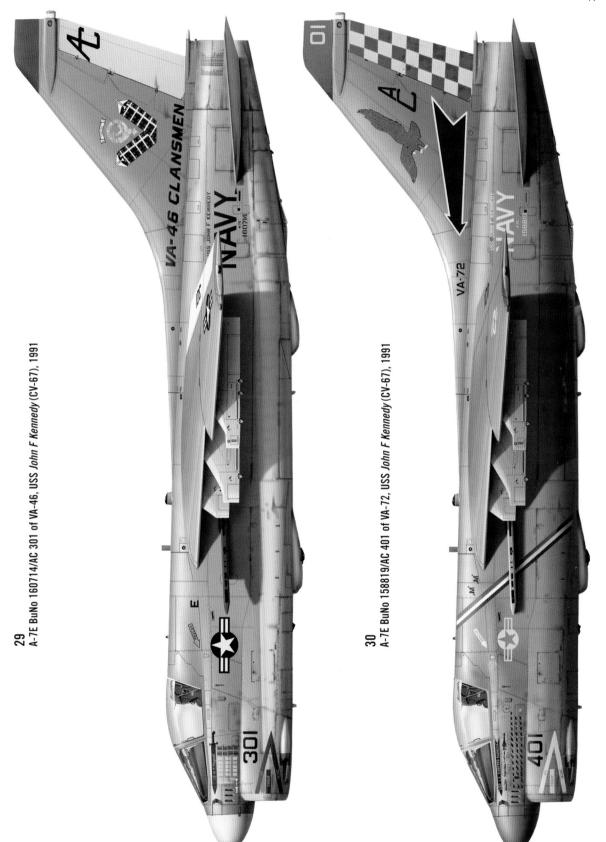

29
A-7E BuNo 160714/AC 301 of VA-46, USS *John F Kennedy* (CV-67), 1991

30
A-7E BuNo 158819/AC 401 of VA-72, USS *John F Kennedy* (CV-67), 1991

As he egressed after dropping his ordnance, Kappel felt his Corsair II shudder as it took a hit in the tail from an SA-7. With his three division lieutenants following him, the XO was able to fly back to the carrier and trap. Later inspection revealed his jet's shredded vertical tail and engine tail cone.

Shortly thereafter, Cdr Duff and CAG Andrews rolled in through a cloud of 57 mm AAA smoke and started their dive toward the target. Some estimates state that 40 shoulder-launched SAMs and fire from 150 AAA guns filled the air with flame and smoke during the entire attack. Duff later declared 'It was like a carpet it was so thick'. Andrews was also in awe of the reception that had awaited the strike aircraft, as he explained in an article he wrote for US Navy publication *Approach* in December 1987;

'In 19 years of flying, I've seen a bit of combat: Vietnam (downtown Hanoi is lovely when the SAMs light off), off the Israeli coast in 1967 and 1973, flying CAP [Combat Air Patrols], during the Iranian hostage exchange and playing tag with Khaddafi's [Gaddafi] fighters in 1981. Yeah, I've seen a lot, but damn, I've never seen so many SAMs! They're all headed for us! Everybody and his brother must have a bottle rocket. The ZSU-23-4s are mesmerizing. They are like golden hoses, streaming lead up toward the incoming bombers.'

Andrews called out the missiles, giving Duff time to evade them but not enough to do so himself. As the CO of VA-15 pulled off to the left to avoid the storm of missiles, he heard CAG call that he had been hit (it was determined his jet had been struck by either an SA-7 or the much-improved SA-9, examples of which had only recently been acquired by the Syrians).

'I just took a hit! I'm on fire!', Andrews noted in his article. 'The airplane's not responding. I've got to get out now! No, wait – I'm still over the mountains. Who knows who's waiting down there for me if I punch out. If I can get the A-7 out over the water I've got a better chance of being rescued by friendlies. Okay, settle down and get the RAT [ram air turbine, which would give him temporary power to keep control of his aircraft] deployed. The airplane's responding and I've got control again. At least I can direct it.'

However, his aircraft was already breaking apart into two sections, and as he rolled left toward the beach, Andrews tried to plan his coming ejection – his third, having previously ejected from an F-8 and an F-14 after they had both suffered serious inflight mechanical failures. Looking back over his left shoulder, he could see his strike group heading to the west, away from the action. The sky was filled with more AAA and SAM smoke.

'Now, 4500 ft above the Shouf Mountains in Lebanon, there's silence where my engine should be. Obviously, I'm riding on borrowed time. If I can just get out over the water.' But Andrews' A-7 started to roll violently to the left. He stomped hard on the right rudder and pulled right on the control column. At about 2500 ft, the aircraft's nose pitched up and started to tumble. 'Suddenly, the burning tail drops off [right behind the wing] and the forward fuselage, with me inside, begins to tumble end-over-end. This is it! My options are gone. I call "'Hunyak's out of here", pull the face curtain of the ejection seat down and shoot out of the Corsair II.'

CAG Andrews had ejected almost at the last moment before the stricken jet quit flying. The remnants of the A-7 headed inland to crash into a house in Zouk Mikael, 12 miles northeast of Beirut International

Airport, injuring a mother and her three children asleep inside – one of the occupants later died. Days later, Cdr Duff was helicoptered out to the crash site to see the remains of the house and oversee the recovery of any classified items from the A-7.

Andrews, who had spent only seven seconds over his target, now hung under his parachute. 'I got a good chute', he reported to *Naval Aviation News* magazine in a post-action interview from his hospital bed, 'and started going through the routine [inflating the life preserver, etc.]. I was over land, but closer to the water than if I'd punched out right after being hit. I decided that heading for the water was the best way to go, and at about the same time I looked up and saw the four-line release for steering the chute hanging over my head. I grabbed them, pulled on one handle and started going inland. I pulled the other handle and started sliding out to sea.'

A Rescue Combat Air Patrol (RESCAP) was immediately launched from CV-62 consisting of two more VA-15 jets. One of them, BuNo 160738, was, ironically, the squadron's 'CAG bird' with Andrews' name on the canopy rail.

CAG hit the water yards away from a small fishing boat manned by an old man and his very young son. At first, Andrews did not want to get into the boat, but the old man kept motioning towards him and CAG climbed aboard. When he told the two Lebanese fishermen he was an American, the old man pulled out a cross from around his neck and said 'Christian!' As they headed for shore, Andrews saw a very fast speedboat, later identified as a *Ski Nautique*, coming toward them. He placed his 0.357 Magnum pistol on the boat's gunnels in case they were enemy soldiers in the speedboat, but they turned out to be Frenchmen who gestured for Andrews to come over to them. He did so, and then transferred to an outboard rubber raft manned by two men in uniform when he got closer to shore because of the shallow water that was too much to accommodate the speedboat's draft. They quickly took him ashore, where a waiting Lebanese army helicopter flew him to a nearby headquarters for examination. A US Marine Corps CH-46 picked him up shortly thereafter and took him to *Independence*, where he was greeted by the captain and deck crew some four hours after launching from the carrier.

Some 24,000 lbs of ordnance – including 12 CBU-59s and 28 Rockeye – had been dropped by the six attacking Corsair IIs that morning, and although the complete target set had been engaged by strikes from both carriers, the bomb damage inflicted was difficult to assess. While the results had officially been described as 'effective', professionally, the event was viewed as nothing short of a failure. This would eventually lead to a number of significant changes within US naval aviation, including the formation of the Naval Strike Warfare Center (soon nicknamed 'Strike University', or 'Strike U') at NAS Fallon, Nevada, to develop and teach more effective air wing tactics.

Cdr – later Capt – Ed 'Hunyak' Andrews, CAG-6, enjoys a surprise visit from famed country singer Loretta Lynn just hours after ejecting from his stricken A-7. Ms Lynn had been touring various ships steaming off the Lebanese coast when she heard the radio sequence of Andrews' ejection and rescue, and she wanted to see him as he rested in 'Indy's' infirmary. Obviously, both are enjoying the impromptu encounter *(US Navy)*

The most important change was the fact that aircraft would no longer fly into potentially hostile airspace during the hours of daylight at medium altitude without dedicated Suppression of Enemy Air Defences (SEAD) support and the emerging AGM-88 High-speed Anti-Radiation Missile (HARM) – both a role and a weapon that A-7 units were soon to embrace. In fact, on 5 October 1981, an AGM-88A had been fired from a Pacific Missile Test Center A-7E based at NAS Point Mugu, California, against a target vessel in the first live warhead launch.

Ironically, the Lebanon mission could have been undertaken at night by CVW-3 and CVW-6, as both the A-6E and A-7E had the technology available to them to hit targets using the cloak of darkness and stealthier ingress tactics. The Intruders were fitted with the Target Recognition and Attack Multisensor (TRAM) housed in a small undernose turret, which allowed crews to employ laser-guided bombs with clinical precision or calculate target slant ranges for accurate dumb bomb release. As previously noted, the A-7Es were equipped with the AN/AAR-45 FLIR pod, which projected a green view of the outside world directly onto the pilot's Head-Up Display. As with the TRAM, it effectively turned night into day.

The loss of two aircraft and two experienced aircrew – one fatally – to man-portable SAMs was a particular driver of tactical change. This aspect of the operation was addressed in a 'quick-reaction' news story in the 12 December 1983 issue of the magazine *Aviation Week & Space Technology*;

'Modification to Soviet-built surface-to-air missile infrared sensors that caused the loss of a Navy/Vought [sic] A-7 and a Grumman A-6E during a December 4 attack on Syrian military positions in Lebanon is forcing the US to evaluate countermeasures. The SA-7 and SA-9 missiles may have

VA-15 CO Cdr Byron Duff (far left) and US Marines visit the crash site of CAG Andrews' A-7 at Zouk Mikael, 12 miles northeast of Beirut International Airport. Duff, who oversaw the recovery of any classified items from the downed jet, had led the strike on the nearby Stentor radar site. Cdr Andrews had flown as his 'dash two' on the mission (*US Navy*)

A section of well-weathered A-7Es from VA-87 patrol off Beirut in 1983-84, both aircraft being armed with single Mk 20 Rockeye canisters on station 8. The city's extremely crowded layout partially explains its occasional description as the 'Paris of the Middle East' (*US Navy*)

had altered wavelengths or filters that allowed them to home directly onto the exhausts of attacking aircraft.'

When questioned about the shoulder-launched SAMs, retired Vice Admiral Mazach commented in an e-mail to the author;

'I never heard about any changes to the SA-7 or SA-9 missiles either before the strike or after. Since both are IR [infrared] heat-seekers, it certainly would not have made a great deal of difference to aircrews in the A-7s or the A-6s. Those missiles have little effect on a fast-moving jet, and thus were used primarily in the target area in this case against jets that were engaged in trying to find gun emplacements and other minimally viable and visible targets, where they posed more of a threat, and had some success.

'This information was not known to the strike participants before the strike, and knowing about such a change probably would not have altered the outcome of the strike, again based on the actual execution and circumstances surrounding same.'

Commenting on the planning of the mission, Vice Admiral Mazach also noted;

'This strike was not a complicated one as far as tactics were concerned. It involved two air wings from two different ships, so it was coordinated. Other than that, nothing was unusual. The changes to the plan received at the very last minute made by the chain of command outside the Area of Responsibility [AOR] are what made the strike seem to be poorly planned and executed – and perhaps seem complicated. It wasn't complicated until 30 to 60 minutes before launch time. As far as the air wings were concerned, we had some of the best tacticians in the A-7 and A-6 communities that existed at that time. The plan that was never allowed to be flown was sound in every way.'

Other factors – specifically target selection and ToT, both of which went in to building the element of surprise, and dictated the release altitudes and ordnance loads – should have been better considered in the hastily revised planning undertaken by the chain of command outside the AOR. The fact that they were not caused the poor results achieved by the strike. These errors would not be repeated in the next in-force strike, namely Operation *El Dorado Canyon* in April 1986.

The hard fact was that the operation did little or nothing to curtail terrorist activities, with ongoing attacks on UN peacekeepers and kidnappings of US personnel continuing for several more years in Lebanon.

CHAPTER FIVE

LIBYA AND IRAN

Although the 1970s had started calmly in the Mediterranean for US forces, tensions steadily rose as the decade progressed thanks to re-occurring, and escalating, conflicts between Israel and its Arab neighbours. The emergence of terrorist groups backed by various nations in the region would also add a further dimension to US naval operations. One such sponsor of terrorist activity in the West was Libya, which had been ruled by Col Muammar Gaddafi following a coup in 1969. He duly established a revolutionary government that grew increasingly hostile to the USA in particular. His actions would lead to several years of conflict with neighbours and two significant operations involving the A-7.

In 1974 Gaddafi had declared that the Gulf of Sidra – the portion of the Mediterranean south of the 32° 30' north latitude – were sovereign Libyan waters, rendering them off-limits to all other shipping. When the US government refused to accept his claims, the Sixth Fleet found itself as the primary tool to dispute the issue. The US Navy's response was to undertake what were described as 'Freedom of Navigation Operations' (FONOPs) that saw both ships and aircraft routinely operating in the disputed waters. The Libyan military's response to this was initially muted, and it would take seven more years before things really heated up.

In August 1981 F-14As from VF-41 embarked in *Nimitz* downed two Libyan Arab Republic Air Force (LARAF) Su-22 'Fitters' that had attempted to engage the fighters as they flew over the Gulf of Sidra. Instead

A VA-66 A-7E launches an AGM-45 Shrike anti-radiation missile during a training mission near Puerto Rico prior to the unit's 1983 cruise on board 'Ike' with CVW-7. Used in great number by A-7 squadrons performing the 'Iron Hand' mission during the latter stages of the conflict in Vietnam, the Shrike's final operational employment by the Corsair II came during Operations *Prairie Fire* and *El Dorado Canyon* in March-April 1986, when VA-72 fired multiple rounds at Libyan fire-detection radar sites (*US Navy*) of directly challenging the US Navy in the wake of what the Libyans viewed as American aggression, Gaddafi's response was to support terrorist attacks in Lebanon and Europe by surrogate groups funded and armed by his regime. In January 1986 President Reagan declared that Libya was an 'unusual and extraordinary' threat to the USA, and it had to be dealt with. At that time Sixth Fleet controlled two carrier battlegroups, USS *Saratoga* (CV-60) (CVW-17 embarked, with VA-81 and VA-83) having just returned from the Indian Ocean, and *Coral Sea* (CVW-13 embarked, which was a new air wing giving the F/A-18A its operational debut with Sixth Fleet – there were no A-7s embarked) having been on station for several weeks. Back in Norfolk, USS *America* (CV-66) (CVW-1 embarked, with VA-46 and VA-72) was preparing for a March departure to join them.

Operation *Attain Document*, a large FONOP, started on 15 January. In direct response to this development, Libya placed its forces on 'full alert' and declared that America was 'practicing state terrorism against a small, peaceful country'. As had happened several times in the past, fighter aircraft from both sides engaged each other over the Gulf of Sidra but there were no shots exchanged this time. A month later, on 12 February, Sixth Fleet returned to the Gulf of Sidra for *Attain Document II*, its vessels sailing across what had now been dubbed 'The Line of Death' due to Gaddafi's frequently dire statements about what would happen to warships that crossed it. The two A-7 squadrons embarked in *Saratoga* were kept busy throughout this period undertaking SUCAP missions and providing tanker support for the other jets in CVW-17.

Attain Document III, which started on 24 March, now included the recently arrived *America* and its battlegroup, increasing Sixth Fleet's strength to 26 warships and 250 aircraft. At 1452 hrs local time on the 24th, the AEGIS radar-equipped cruiser USS *Yorktown* (CG-48) alerted a fighter CAP of two VF-102 F-14As operating more than 50 miles off the coast of Libya that two SA-5 SAMs had been launched at them from a site near the Libyan town of Sirte. No fewer than five missiles (four SA-5s and an SA-2) are believed to have been fired in that salvo. All were thwarted with aggressive manoeuvring by the F-14 crews, combined with effective jamming by supporting EA-6Bs.

The fire-detection radar site at Sirte responsible for the SA-5 launches was subsequently the target of three separate attacks by anti-radiation missile-armed strike aircraft from *America* and *Saratoga* after it became active again at 2200 hrs local time. Amongst the jets to target the site were four A-7Es

VA-81's 'Sunliner 407' is pre-flighted by its pilot while chained down to the flightdeck of CV-60 in March 1986. The Corsair II is armed with a single AGM-45 and two Mk 20 Rockeye canisters, as well as a pair of AIM-9Ls – it is also carrying a solitary 300-gal tank. An F-14A from VF-74 is parked behind the A-7E, it too being fully armed with AIM-9Ls and AIM-7M air-to-air missiles (*US Navy*)

from VA-83, two of which were equipped with AGM-88A HARM rounds. The first pair, led by DCAG Cdr R G Brodsky, approached Sirte at high altitude to divert the operators' attention before breaking off, while two more Corsair IIs headed for the site at an altitude of less than 500 ft and launched a pair of AGM-88As – the first operational use of the new HARM in combat. One weapon missed, but the second missile reportedly demolished a radar antenna, putting the site out of action for four hours.

Early the following morning, when the Sirte radar site became active once again, it was VA-46's turn to use two HARM rounds in what proved to be one of the last attacks of this brief operation – codenamed *Prairie Fire* – which also saw A-6s sink two Libyan warships and badly damage a third. These strikes were deemed to be adequate response options by Sixth Fleet as the rules of engagement had been satisfied following Libya firing upon US forces. No US aircraft had been damaged during the operation, despite several SAM launches (predominantly SA-2s) from sites at Sirte and Benghazi. A total of 1546 sorties had been flown by aircraft from the three carriers, 375 of them south of 'The Line of Death'. Furthermore, vessels from the battlegroups had sailed with impunity in the Gulf of Sidra for three days, before withdrawing north.

The pilot of an A-7E from VA-83, embarked in *Saratoga*, inspects the nose gear launch bar of his aircraft on 24 March 1986. The jet is armed with at least one AGM-88A HARM, replacement for the AGM-45 Shrike in the SEAD mission. VA-83 would give the weapon its operational debut during the evening of 24 March, when two HARMs were fired at a fire-detection radar site at Sirte that had been responsible for a SAM attack on F-14s from VF-102 earlier that same day (*US Navy*)

Having strapped into their A-7s, pilots from VA-81 and VA-83 await engine start up from yellow power carts on 22 March 1986. Two days later Corsair IIs targeted Libyan fire-detection radar sites near Sirte, with VA-81 flying decoy missions and VA-83 firing AGM-88A HARMs. *Saratoga* was nearing the end of seventh-month deployment when it participated in *Prairie Fire*, hence the weathered appearance of CVW-17's aircraft in this photograph (*US Navy*)

EL DORADO CANYON

Shortly after *Prairie Fire*, and despite the likelihood of further action, Sixth Fleet permitted *Saratoga* to withdraw on 30 March to leave the battlegroups of *America* and *Coral Sea* on station in the Mediterranean. On 5 April a West Berlin discotheque frequented by US military personnel was bombed, resulting in the deaths of three people (including one American serviceman) and leaving more than 220 injured, 74 of them US citizens. The Reagan Administration soon declared it had incontrovertible evidence (derived from British signals intelligence) of Libya's involvement, and this in turn led to the President authorising air strikes – Operation *El Dorado Canyon* was to be executed over the night of 14/15 April. The USAF wanted to be included in

Only a fraction of CVW-1's embarked strength can be seen in this overhead view of *America* taken by a TARPS-equipped Tomcat from VF-102 during the early stages of the carrier's 1986 Mediterranean deployment. Indeed, just nine of the 24 A-7Es from VA-46 and VA-72 are visible (*US Navy*)

this operation, so British-based F-111F bombers, plus electronic warfare and tanker assets, joined with US Navy forces to deliver a series of significant strikes on Libyan government and military installations.

For much of the day on 14 April, the *America* battlegroup operated under strict emissions control status so as not to reveal their location as they moved around the west of Sicily and between Tunisia and Malta to take up position ahead of midnight. Amongst the aircraft launched from the carrier between 0045 and 0120 hrs local time on the 15th were six A-7Es drawn from both VA-46 and VA-72, these aircraft joining with strike assets from *Coral Sea* to form an aerial armada from both ships that worked in coordination with their USAF counterparts flying non-stop from Britain. ToT for all of the bombers was 0200 hrs local time.

Lt Cdr Carroll White, who had never fired an AGM-45 at night before, was one of the three VA-72 Shrike 'shooters' during the strike. Although his unit was particularly aware of the SA-5 threat posed by the Libyans, VA-72 did not consider the SAM a problem because of the low altitude the bombers would be flying at and the very long-range, medium-to-high altitude missile's lack of manoeuvrability. However, White and his fellow Naval Aviators were concerned about the Crotale system, and they intended to stay far enough off the coast in order to remain out of range of the French-built SAM.

The dilemma facing VA-72 was how to get close enough to loft-launch the Shrike, which did not have a long range, and hit the SA-3 sites inland that the unit had been tasked with neutralising, while staying outside any possible Crotale threat ring. The latter was a short-range, highly mobile system that the Libyans could have realistically positioned right on the beach. The A-7 pilots planned to approach the coastline at low altitude and shoot their Shrikes while Prowlers from VMAQ-2 Det Yankee (also assigned to CVW-1) provided jamming coverage behind them.

As squadron CO Cdr Fields Richardson, along with Lt Cdrs Randy Robb and Carroll White, prepared to move up to *America*'s catapults for an 0100 hrs launch, Robb's aircraft went down on the flightdeck, requiring the spare, flown by Lt A J Rizzo, to take its place. Each A-7E carried four AGM-45s without external fuel tanks, and two Sidewinders for use against possible LARAF interceptors (no Libyan aircraft were seen that night). As previously noted, their targets were SA-3 sites and their 'Low Blow' radar that could pose a threat to the inbound F-111s.

Using pre-emptive launch tactics, the A-7Es began firing both AGM-45 Shrikes (VA-72 expended eight) and AGM-88 HARM (VA-46 launched 16) at 0154 hrs to take out Libyan radar assets, including those used by SA-2, SA-3, SA-6, SA-8 and French Crotale missile sites protecting Tripoli

and Benghazi. Any SAMs that were fired from surviving launchers were reported as being unguided, and the Sirte site hit twice in March only went active as the attack waves egressed the target.

Having cleared a path for the bombers, USAF F-111s hit Tripoli-area targets while the A-6Es headed for Benghazi as part of the pre-planned deconfliction of the strike packages. Amongst the sites hit by aircraft from the two carriers were a military barracks suspected of containing a possible terrorist command and control facility hosted by the elite Jamahiriyah ('State of the Masses') Guard and a LARAF overhaul depot for MiG and Sukhoi fighters. All US Navy strike aircraft were 'feet wet' by 0213 hrs, and *America*'s jets – including all six A-7s – had recovered aboard by 0253 hrs.

The only aircraft lost during the operation was an F-111F from the 48th Tactical Fighter Wing, which was possibly downed by either a shoulder-launched SAM or AAA as it attacked its target in Tripoli. As they made their way back to *America*, the A-7 pilots had seen the F-111s pass beneath them in full afterburner, inbound to their targets. Lt Cdr White subsequently reported;

'I was in a section of A-7Es carrying AGM-45 Shrike missiles targeting two SA-3 sites along the Libyan coast between Sidi Bilal and Tripoli. On my third run when ten nautical miles from the beach at around 0202 or 0203 hrs, I observed a fireball at about my level (500-800 ft) to my right toward the vicinity of Sidi Bilal. The fireball went from right to left and appeared to impact the water close to the beach. I observed no seat/ capsule rockets [the F-111 used an escape capsule] and heard no voice transmissions or emergency beeper. I remained within 15 miles of the beach for the next 15 minutes and heard or saw no indications that the aircrew had escaped.'

The crew of the F-111, Capt Fernando Ribas-Dominicci (pilot) and Capt Paul Lorence (Weapon Systems Operator), perished when their jet hit the water.

VA-46's 'Tartan 306', armed with three AGM-88As, is seconds away from launching from CV-66 during the early hours of 15 April 1986. Six A-7Es from VA-46 and VA-72 departed the carrier between 0045 and 0120 hrs local time to provide SEAD support for Operation *El Dorado Canyon*. The Corsair IIs from VA-46 were armed with HARMs and the jets from VA-72 used Shrikes. The Prowler awaiting its turn to launch from waist catapult four was one of the VMAQ-2 Det Yankee jets that provided jamming coverage behind the Corsair IIs during their attacks on Libyan radar and SAM sites (*US Navy*)

Although the US Navy quickly stated that *El Dorado Canyon* had achieved its limited objectives, the US State Department subsequently confirmed Gaddafi was continuing to support international terrorism – including the destruction of a Pan American Airlines Boeing 747 over Scotland on 21 December 1988. The loss of a UTA DC-10 over Chad in September of the following year was also traced to Libyan agents. Despite these events, the US government still asserted that 'the United States had not only the means but the will to deal effectively with international terrorism'.

The pilot of VA-46's 'Tartan 304' prepares to get the launch signal from *America*'s catapult officer, known as the 'shooter', during flight operations off Libya's coast in April 1986. The Corsair II carries HARM and Mk 20 Rockeye, as well as at least one AIM-9L (*US Navy*)

WAR AT SEA

While Sixth Fleet kept a close eye on Libya, other carriers continued making long deployments to the Indian Ocean to monitor Iran in the wake of the 1979 revolution. Practically every carrier assigned to Seventh Fleet (both Atlantic and Pacific Fleet vessels) spent time in the Indian Ocean between 1980 and 1990. These cruises were typically long and monotonous for crews, with few liberty ports to break things up. Logistical support also remained a challenge. Meanwhile, the US Navy continued to develop the militarised atoll of Diego Garcia (an overseas territory of the United Kingdom), just south of the equator in the central Indian Ocean, as a forward support base. It also worked with friendly local governments – generally those threatened by Iran – for improved facility access.

VA-72's 'Decoy 401' (BuNo 160549) has its instrument panel checked by maintenance personnel on 19 April 1986. It is armed with the standard SEAD loadout for this period – HARM (or, in the case of VA-72, Shrike) and Mk 20 Rockeye. *America*'s involvement in FONOPs off Libya took place at the very start of its sixth-month deployment with Sixth Fleet, hence the clean appearance of this aircraft (*US Navy*)

Tensions in the Arabian Gulf (known as the Persian Gulf to US service personnel) region had steadily risen since the start of the Iran-Iraq war in September 1980. While the two nations were engaged in a bloody eight-year conflict, the Western powers (and the United States in particular) attempted to keep the Strait of Hormuz and Arabian Gulf open for tanker traffic. By 1987 the Islamic Republic of Iran Navy was laying mines throughout the gulf, which resulted in several skirmishes between US and Iranian Revolutionary Guard units. On 14 April 1988 the frigate USS *Samuel B Roberts* (FFG-58) hit an Iranian mine and was heavily damaged. Four days later, the US Navy initiated Operation *Praying Mantis* as a response to Iranian actions. The centrepiece to this action would be the *Enterprise* battlegroup and, specifically, the Intruders (VA-95) and Corsair IIs (VA-22 and VA-94) of CVW-11.

Amongst the Naval Aviators involved in *Praying Mantis* was

VA-94's Lt Tom Ganse, who was the pilot of the first jet launched off *Enterprise* on the morning of 18 April. Here, he provides some background to the War At Sea, and details of his mission;

'From a global perspective, the US military was still recovering from the psychological backlash of the Vietnam conflict and President Jimmy Carter's appeasement policy in the Middle East, compounded by ageing equipment and an insufficient infrastructure. The Reagan build-up was in full swing by 1988, and the future was looking bright. Still, there hadn't been much of a chance to test our mettle other than in Operation *El Dorado Canyon*. Against it all, the Cold War was reaching a climax. All this led to a national strategy that emphasised freedom of navigation – the ability to transit international waters and airspace anywhere, anytime. This meant we regularly challenged any and all belligerent claims to extended borders, such as Iran's attempt to control the Strait of Hormuz which prompted the instigation of Operation *Earnest Will* – the American military protection of Kuwaiti-owned tankers.

'The latter commenced in late July 1987, and it had proven very successful in subduing the harassment and attacks against shipping passing through the Strait. Along with *Earnest Will*, regular minesweeping operations substantially reduced the effectiveness of the Iranian mining campaign – until *Samuel B Roberts* hit a mine on 14 April 1988.

'*Enterprise* and CVW-11 had been scheduled to transit to the Diego Garcia operating area for a week of employing live ordnance in a training environment dubbed "Weapons Week". This was part of something called a non-combat expenditure allowance (NCEA), which allowed aircrew to experience the real thing, while also providing a quality assurance check on ordnance supplies. We knew that was off the calendar as soon as we heard the *Roberts* had hit the mine, the battlegroup being told to remain in the North Arabian Sea/Gulf of Oman. Now, an opportunity had presented itself to use the "Weapons Week" ordnance against a target that might actually shoot back.

'I think we all knew there would be a military response, most likely naval, and that there was a high probability it would involve elements of CVW-11. Bear in mind, the last retaliatory strike was *El Dorado Canyon*, and that was for a bomb at a disco. Most of us figured the *Roberts* was more important than a disco, so we were expecting, and preparing for, the call to visit downtown Tehran. There wasn't much going on but fevered speculation over the next 48 hours or so, until word came down on the 17th that we would provide a "measured response" by destroying the oil platform hosting mine-laying operations and taking out one of their frigates in exchange for the *Roberts*.

'It was interesting to see how the tone changed when we got the official word that there would be combat, especially among the previously unindoctrinated. Funny how the loudest mouths became the most quiet

Lt Tom Ganse, who was the pilot of the first jet launched off *Enterprise* on the morning of the War At Sea, poses with A-7E 'Hobo 401' (BuNo 159989) at NAS Lemoore in early 1987. His left foot is resting on the retractable two-step ladder used by the pilot to gain access to the cockpit. Two pull-out footholds above the ladder were also utilised. Ganse flew Corsair IIs with both VA-94 and VA-113 and F/A-18C Hornets with VFA-94 (*US Navy*)

as they came to grips with the concept that they might very well have to deal with someone shooting to kill. At that point, no one knew exactly who would be assigned what, but this was to be a politically correct event and every interest would be represented.

'Eventually, we learned that there would be a War At Sea strike package assembled and put on alert to launch as soon as the frigate *Sabalan* [which had been attacking merchant ships in the area] was located. Everyone else would participate in CAPs, whether against SUCAP or enemy fighters [MiGCAP or BARCAP]. This was standard fare during *Earnest Will* operations, but on the 18th we would dramatically enhance the number of CAPs to effectively cover both sides of the Strait. On a CAP, of course, you are armed and ready, should anything come into your "zone" and demonstrate hostile intent.

'CVW-11's principal strike aircraft for a War At Sea were VA-95's A-6Es armed with AGM-84 Harpoon and AGM-123B Skipper II anti-ship missiles, Laser-Guided Bombs (LGBs) and Mk 20 Rockeye, while the A-7Es of VA-22 and VA-94 would carry [AGM-62] Walleye II glide bombs, Mk 20 Rockeye and "slick" Mk 83 dumb bombs. Any of these weapons were potentially bad news for an enemy ship from the Soviet Navy [against whom they were designed to be employed], but a strike group employing all of these "punches" against a rogue nation was akin to killing ants with blowtorches.

'The War At Sea package was established as a section of two A-6s and three A-7s each from VA-22 and VA-94. The reason for the third Corsair II from each squadron was that this aircraft would be equipped with an AN/AWW-9B datalink pod to control the Walleye II TV-guided glide bomb carried by one of the other A-7s in the flight. With all that set, the squadron COs faced the difficult dilemma of deciding who would fly which missions. As it turned out, the way events unfolded the following day made all that angst unnecessary.

'As the senior lieutenant in the squadron, and with a 3-in-17 chance of drawing the War At Sea, I thought I'd be a natural selection. Instead, the

An A-7E of the Naval Strike Warfare Center (nicknamed 'Strike University' or 'Strike U') carries a CATM-62 (Captive Air Training Missile) Walleye II ER/DL glide bomb over one of the ranges at its NAS Fallon home during the 1980s. Developed from the original AGM-62 Walleye precision-guided weapon of the Vietnam War, the AGM-62B Walleye II became operational with US Navy Corsair II units in 1976 and was used in limited numbers during both Operations *Praying Mantis* and *Desert Storm* (*US Navy*)

Skipper [Cdr "Tad" Chamberlain] pulled me aside to tell me he specifically did not select me for several reasons, one of which was the fact that I was already extended past my rotation date in order to augment *Earnest Will* ops. He didn't want to risk having to send a letter to my next of kin when I shouldn't have been there to begin with. My consolation prizes were that I would be scheduled to fly twice on 18 April (I would ultimately fly three times over the course of the operation) and have the distinction of being the first jet to launch, thus opening *Praying Mantis*.

'Now, about that distinction. One might think the first jet to launch would have a pretty glamorous role, but this would not be the case on the 18th. Like the first (American) football player to move, there isn't much glamour in being a football Center. And there isn't much glamour in launching off in a "KA-7E" tanker, even if it is loaded with two AIM-9M heat-seeking missiles and 1000 rounds of 20 mm ammo. But there I was in my "Combat Tanker", climbing as expeditiously as possible on my all-important mission of checking that the assigned USAF KC-10 tanker was "sweet" (able to transfer fuel).

'All hands waited anxiously on deck for me to make the call. "Sweet tanker" meant the fight was on, while "Sour tanker" meant disaster. What would it be? The tanker gods smiled upon us that early morning and the "Big E" swung into action, hurtling aircraft into the skies over the Gulf of Oman as I proceeded onto my secondary mission as a Barrier CAP [BARCAP] between *Enterprise* and the Iranian F-4 base at Chabahar. Right! No air-to-air radar in the A-7, but it wasn't hard to see an old F-4 coming your way – to be fair, the AIM-9M does have an all-aspect capability, so, in theory, I had a fighting chance during a head-on engagement with an afterburner-belching F-4. With my jet also carrying two 2000-lb drop tanks and a D-704 inflight "buddy" refuelling pod, I mused upon whether I was there to shoot down potential transgressors or refuel the thirsty Iranian fighters!

'On a more serious note, there was nothing about our operations at this point that would appear unusual to the Iranians, and we had the E-2 airborne to provide vectors and authorisation to engage if required. Alas, no one wanted to play that early in the day, and with the first launch cycle

Lt Tom Ganse of VA-94 holds 'Hobo 407' (BuNo 160731) in close formation with his section leader during a training sortie in February 1986 while *Enterprise* was transiting the Pacific on its way to the Indian Ocean. The aircraft carries an empty TER (used to carry lightweight Mk 76 or Mk 106 practice bombs), an AIM-9L and an AN/AWW-9B datalink pod to control a Walleye II glide bomb carried by another A-7. The Walleye had an electro-optical seeker in its nose and a datalink to transmit the image back to the controlling aircraft. Walleye training involved having the pilot of the A-7 carrying the CATM-62 fly the weapon flight profile from 'release' to target overflight while the jet with the pod relayed steering commands (*US Navy*) completed, I'd been relieved on station by a section of eminently more capable F-14s. After topping them off, I returned to *Enterprise* and landed shortly after the completion of the initial launch cycle, thus bringing to an end the first successful mission of *Praying Mantis*.'

One of the pilots in the vanguard of the action on 18 April was the CO of VA-94, Cdr Carl W 'Tad' Chamberlain;

'The *Praying Mantis* War At Sea took place before the carrier battlegroups sailed into the Persian Gulf, so we were positioned in the North Arabian Sea. We had a lot of contingency targets assigned in and around the Persian Gulf, and we regularly flew in the area to demonstrate our presence. This was during the tanker escort operations [Operation *Earnest Will*], and one of the main threats to the tankers were Iranian Silkworm surface-to-surface missiles that were positioned along the coast south of Bandar Abbas. These were a threat to both tankers and warships. We had worked out tactics to deliver Walleye IIs and hard-nosed bombs into the tunnels the Iranians used to shelter the Silkworm missiles, so I'd had Walleye on my mind for a long time.

'One night I was hanging out, watching the movie in the ready room, when CVW-11's CAG, Capt [Louis R] "Bullet Bob" Canepa, came down and asked me "Do you want to lead a strike tomorrow?" I said, "Yeah, sure" – more likely I jumped to my feet and said "yessir!" At the time I thought it was another practice mission, but CAG added "This is the real deal". CVW-11 had been directed to sink a particular Iranian frigate [the Saam-class vessel *Sabalan*] that had been stopping tankers in the Strait of Hormuz, checking their cargo and where they were headed, and then, as the frigate pulled away, it would spray the merchant ship with machine gun fire. President Reagan learned of the situation, said it was the second time he'd heard about this ship and its crew doing that, and he ordered them sunk.

'CAG had established several teams within the air wing to plan strikes and develop tactics, and as skipper of VA-94 I was in charge of one of those teams. We had someone on the team from all the warfare specialties and had planned many strikes together in all the various warfare areas, so when we got tapped to hit this frigate we were able to quickly put together a good tactical plan by picking from some of our past tactics that had proven successful.

A 'KA-7E' from VA-22 provides fuel via a D-704 inflight buddy refuelling pod to an A-6E from VA-95 during CVW-11's one-day War At Sea against Iranian naval vessels on 18/19 April 1988. The Corsair II had a good internal fuel capacity and the ability to loiter for a long time, allowing it to carry a considerable amount of fuel for offload. Typically, the D-704 (which also contained some fuel) would be carried on the outer port wing pylon, and its weight counterbalanced by two 300-gal fuel tanks on the starboard side (*US Navy*)

'I chose the Extended Range Data Link [ERDL] Walleye II as the weapon of choice for the A-7 because it would put a lot of explosive power on the target with its 2000-lb linear-shaped charge warhead. Furthermore, it could be guided to a precision aim point with the AN/AWW-9B datalink pod, while also providing significant standoff delivery in the event the target could muster some surface-to-air defence. The datalink pod would also provide us with recorded video of the Walleye's flight, but only if the pod itself worked – having practiced with the weapon a lot, we knew that they were notoriously unreliable. Nevertheless, there was a good chance of an accurate hit even if the datalink failed.

'We had been given the ASuW [anti-surface warfare] mission to sink the *Sahand* [sister-ship of *Sabalan*]. The frigate had already suffered a near miss by an LGB and single hits from a Harpoon and a Skipper II, all of these weapons having been expended by a single A-6. It would also be hit by another Harpoon fired by one of our surface warships [USS *Joseph Strauss* (DDG-16)]. Now it was the A-7s' job to finish her off – just inflicting more damage wasn't going to cut it. We knew the ship had been damaged somewhat, but didn't know for sure what surface-to-air threat might still exist, so the standoff capability of the ERDL Walleye was key.

'The attack element of the strike had six A-7s, three from my squadron and three from VA-22. The formation consisted of three sections, with each section in combat spread, and sections two and three a couple of miles in trail of the section ahead. The first section had Walleye IIs and a pair of slick Mk 83s, the second section carried the data link pods and Mk 83s and the third section was the "clean-up crew" carrying only Mk 83s. I designed the formation in this way so that everybody got maximum time in their run for precise aiming. We really wanted good hits.

'The idea was for the first section to release their Walleyes from a standoff range, then continue on to the target with their Mk 83s. Same for the second section, who would datalink the Walleyes after release, then continue in with their Mk 83s. Finally, the last section would back up the whole effort with yet another two pairs of Mk 83s. This way, if all went as planned, we'd put lots of "boom" onto the target, but even if we got scattered by some defensive fire, we would still have the two big Walleyes on their way being guided by the datalinks from a standoff distance.

'One of my big concerns was targeting the right ship among the traffic that's always transiting the strait along there. The last thing I wanted to happen was for us to line up on the wrong ship and have to abort the run, turn around and regroup. As always, the great E-2 had the situation well in hand. They not only kept an eye on any air threat that might try to come feet wet, but they had the surface picture down cold. As soon as we got into the area, they vectored us exactly onto *Sahand*, and confirmed that the area around her was clear of other shipping. Our fighter buddies had us covered too. They set up a couple of racetrack sections which kept one plane always facing the beach to lock up any bad guys who might poke their nose our way.

'We got visual on the target a good way out, and identified it easily with the magnified Walleye view. It was a smooth delivery, with an almost

'Hobo 401' (BuNo 159989) is just moments away from riding CVN-65's waist catapult four on 19 April 1988 during *Praying Mantis*, the aircraft carrying at least one 'slick' 500-lb Mk 83 bomb on station eight. Most of the aircraft from VA-22 and VA-94 committed to the War At Sea carried a mixed load of Mk 83s and Walleye IIs, although some of the A-7s had bombs only. All of them carried two AIM-9Ls (*US Navy*)

straight ahead roll in. The first section of jets "whistled down the chute" and released the two Walleyes right on the mark. We were in about a 20-30 degree dive and released at about four miles. This gave us good standoff, while keeping plenty of "smack" [energy] on the gliding Walleyes.

'Lt Cdr [T H] "Hoss" Price was my Walleye guy, and he released with the bomb locked perfectly onto the base of the ship's superstructure. As the bomb glided in, my datalink picture showed the cursor break lock and track along the deck edge toward the bow. My darn datalink wouldn't slew the cursor back to the initial aim point so the bomb hit forward on the forecastle. Cdr [William] "Grits" Roberson, skipper of VA-22, got a great hit with the other Walleye. In his words, "Mine hit the hull just below the forward gun mount, went into the magazine underneath the mount and generated a huge explosion. I put the aim point onto the gun mount and Lt 'Scoop' Roberts moved it down to where it finally went. I had pulled up after my release, and 'Scoop' moved the aim point when I was eyes off the target, but I did get to see the Walleye hit after I had rolled out on top and sneaked a peek."

'The plan was for everyone to make a single run, pull off left and egress back down the strait toward home. Because I had been wrestling with my faulty datalink for so long I didn't have time to switch to bombs and get the Mk 83s off on that first pass, so I pulled off right and climbed to a high-dive roll in for the bombs. My right 270-degree turn gave the section behind me time to get clear, and I figured if I didn't see any defensive fire by the time I got to the roll in I'd go for it. I did, and was lucky enough to sling the two bombs right down the stack just aft of the ship's bridge.

'I snapped a few handheld 35mm pictures as I jinked away from the target, then we straggled the 80 or 100 miles back to the carrier under the ever watchful eye of the "Hummer" [E-2] and our fighters.

'In the A-7 light attack community, both land targets and War At Sea missions were our bread and butter. However, this is the first and, to my knowledge, only time the A-7 ever performed a real strike mission against a ship with the Walleye II. In practice, missions were frequently flown against US and sometimes allied ships to test their reaction time and self-defence capabilities. We had what was called a PASSEX [passing exercise] where two converging battlegroups would operate against each other. This included reconnaissance missions to locate and track "enemy" ships, as well as offensive War At Sea strikes.

'What the air wings learned from the many PASSEXs was how critical it was to coordinate the strike by commencing with stand-off weapons in order to neutralise any surface-to-air defences ships might have. This would give attack aircraft the chance to achieve success without incurring too many losses. The A-7's only standoff weapons were HARM and Walleye II, and if we tried to use standard tactics with the

Burning profusely after being hit by missiles and bombs, *Sahand* quickly sank after being targeted by both aircraft and surface vessels of the US Navy. The Corsair II pilots hit it twice with AGM-62Bs and multiple times with Mk 82 bombs. The frigate was also hit by two AGM-123 Skipper missiles and an AGM-84 Harpoon launched from a VA-95 A-6E (which also recorded a near-miss on the ship with a 500-lb LGB) and a second Harpoon fired from the destroyer *Joseph Strauss* (*US Navy*)

latter we would likely get our arses shot off. So we tried different tactics like firing both HARM and Walleyes at long range in loft mode to suppress and saturate the target's fire-control radars, which controlled their SAMs and guns. The A-6s with their Harpoons were also a critical part of the air wing's saturation plan.

'When we had to continue in to the target, we did it at very low level with our jets typically armed with Mk 83s, attacking simultaneously from multiple directions to swarm the defenses. The Argentine A-4s used these tactics in the Falklands War of 1982 with some success against Royal Navy ships but, as we learned, they suffered a lot of losses if they got near the target.'

While Cdr Chamberlain was helping to sink *Sahand*, its sister-ship *Sabalan* was detected departing the Iranian port city of Bandar Abbas, and aircraft were despatched to investigate. It was quickly hit by an A-6-delivered 500-lb LGB 'right down the stack', which left the frigate dead in the water. As had been the case with *Sahand*, the ship's crew attempted to defend themselves by firing several infrared-guided SAMs, none of which connected. Additional aircraft (including A-7s) were en route to sink the frigate when the call to 'knock it off' came from the Pentagon. *Sabalan* was towed back into port.

Lt Ganse was airborne again on 19 April, allowing him to add two more green ink entries in his log book, denoting combat missions;

'The second day of *Praying Mantis* was much like the first, as CVW-11 had F-14s in various CAP locations and A-6s and A-7s in various SUCAP "zones", except that the Ayatollah didn't want to play on day two. Meanwhile, the "KA-7E" and KA-6D "bucket brigade" kept the CAPs airborne by shuttling fuel from the KC-10 to the CAP aircraft. I logged 3.9 hours on that flight.

'My final flight was at night in one of the last SUCAP missions before we wrapped up the event. I can't be positive, but I believe the loadout was a Mk 83 1000-lb bomb on each of stations 1, 2, 6, 7 and 8, with a drop tank on station 3, AIM-9s on stations 4 and 5 and a full belt of ammo in the nose for the 20 mm cannon. My CAP was pretty far north in the Strait of Hormuz, with the closest point of approach to Bandar Abbas being just 12 nautical miles away. I found it somewhat entertaining that on every third or fourth inbound leg, the distant sky would light up with tracers from AAA batteries in Bandar Abbas. I suppose they were shooting at me, but I have no idea why at that range. In any event, it was a pretty light show.'

The senior leadership within the US Navy viewed *Praying Mantis* as how to do business when dealing with belligerent foreign powers threatening freedom of navigation in international waters, seeing it as a measure of how much warfighting had improved since the disastrous Lebanon raid of December 1983.

The Naval Aviators from VA-94 gather together for a photograph on the flightdeck of *Enterprise* shortly after *Praying Mantis*. Standing sixth from left is squadron CO Cdr Carl W 'Tad' Chamberlain and in the front row at the extreme right is Lt Tom Ganse (*US Navy*)

CHAPTER SIX

DESERT SHIELD/STORM

The pilot of 'Tartan 301' (BuNo 160714) tucks in close alongside his section lead whilst on a training mission from CV-67 during *Desert Shield*, the aircraft being armed with Mk 82 500-lb slick bombs and AIM-9Ls. Having just crossed the Saudi Arabian coastline from the Red Sea, both jets were heading for a nearby bombing range (*US Navy*)

On 2 August 1990, Iraq invaded its neighbour Kuwait under the pretext of 'protecting' native Iraqis living in the country. The world, and the US in particular, responded swiftly. The initial military action involved one aircraft carrier from each coast, with *Independence* (CVW-14) arriving from WestPac, while the Sixth Fleet provided *Dwight D Eisenhower* (CVW-7), which passed through the Suez Canal to take station in the Red Sea. The 'Indy' would eventually transit the Strait of Hormuz and enter the Arabian Gulf, thus establishing the operational plan that would be used in the coming war. These plans duly took into account grave concerns about operating carriers within the gulf's restricted waters. However, as full-out war approached it became obvious that the US Navy would have to accept the risk in order to get its carriers close enough in the east to be relevant to the campaign that lay ahead.

Back in the USA and Japan, six more carriers and their air wings were quickly prepared to head towards the region to participate in what had now been officially called Operation *Desert Shield*. From the Atlantic Fleet came *Saratoga* (CVW-17) and *John F Kennedy* (CVW-3), *America* (CVW-1) and USS *Theodore Roosevelt* (CVN-71) (CVW-8). The latter two departed the US prior to New Year's Day, with the goal of making a fast transit across the Atlantic and being on station by mid-January. The Pacific Fleet sent *Midway* (CVW-5), which relieved *Independence* in the gulf in mid-December, while USS *Ranger* (CV-61) (CVW-2) sailed from San Diego on 8 December and soon became the second carrier in the gulf.

Only one of these vessels had A-7s embarked, however – 'JFK'. By the late summer of 1990 most light attack squadrons had either been decommissioned or transitioned to the more capable F/A-18 Hornet. The final Pacific Fleet units equipped with the jet, VA-27 and VA-97, had completed the aircraft's last WestPac deployment, on board USS *Carl Vinson* (CVN-70), at the end of July 1990 and were now in the process of switching to Hornets. That left only Atlantic Fleet units VA-37 and VA-105 (of CVW-6), based at NAS Cecil Field, Florida, fully equipped with the A-7. Co-located VA-46 and VA-72 (of CVW-3) had started transferring their Corsair IIs to VA-37 and VA-105 and transitioning to the Hornet when the invasion of Kuwait occurred. CVW-3 was duly ordered on board CV-67 to participate in *Desert Shield* and VA-37 and VA-105 took their place in the F/A-18 transition schedule instead, leaving VA-46 and VA-72 to hastily prepare for war. Cdr (later Admiral) Mark Fitzgerald, CO of VA-46, recalls the rush to get the unit ready to sail after receiving orders to join 'JFK', and then the intensive work-ups undertaken by CVW-3 in the lead up to Operation *Desert Storm*;

'3 August 1990 at Cecil Field was a typical summer's day in Florida. Hot, humid and thunderstorms forecast for the late afternoon. VA-46 and VA-72 had just returned in June from a "love boat cruise" of the Caribbean, Fleet Week New York and Boston in *John F Kennedy*. The squadrons were transitioning to the F/A-18C and about half the pilots and maintainers were in ground school in VFA-106. VA-37 and VA-105 had accepted many of the 12 A-7E aircraft from each squadron. It was Friday and all were looking forward to the weekend.

'But Saddam had invaded Kuwait on 2 August and President Bush was looking for options. CVW-3 CAG Capt Hardin White called me in the early afternoon asking what it would take to reconstitute the squadron and deploy. The only answer was we will do what it takes. We didn't have a deploy order, but the squadrons and Light Attack Wing went into overdrive to be ready to answer the bell. We could muster 16 of 17 pilots, accept the aircraft back that we had just transferred and recall our technicians from VFA-106. It would be an all-hands effort and our Maintenance leadership went into full gear. Working all weekend, we began getting aircraft back, pilots bounced and cruise boxes packed. The official orders to deploy came Monday morning. We were leaving Friday – four days' notice. We were told to plan for a three-month deployment – right! Still needing a 17th pilot, we called NAS Lemoore, California, where the "last A-7 deployment" on *Carl Vinson* had just arrived home. Yes, they had a volunteer, and Lt(jg) Kevin Mannix would arrive Wednesday. On arrival, he asked when he would bounce. Friday, only it would be on *Kennedy*! Welcome to the squadron.

'*Eisenhower* and *Independence* were on station in the [Arabian] Gulf, *Saratoga* had just deployed and we were peddling fast to get to the Middle East. The carriers were the only air power available to stop Saddam from continuing south into the oil fields of Saudi Arabia, and our mission was clear. No port calls, get through "the ditch" (Suez Canal) and relieve *Independence*, which was well past its return date. We got carrier qualified quickly, and headed east through the Mediterranean, where we used Italian

John F Kennedy heads across the Atlantic at the start of its seven-month-long deployment in August 1990. With CVW-3 embarked, the ship sailed in the Red Sea for the duration of *Desert Shield/Desert Storm*, as did *Saratoga* and *America* – all were part of Battle Force Yankee/TF-155 (*US Navy*)

and Greek target ranges to get CVW-3 back up to speed, then through "the ditch" into the Red Sea.

'On arrival, diplomatic posturing was well underway, and it appeared we were in for a long waiting period. The flying was superb, using northern Saudi Arabia as our training grounds with the famous "Star Wars Canyon" [not to be confused with a similarly nicknamed canyon in Oman] and wonderful low levels.

'Our "mature" A-7s had all of the latest gear. Our HARM system was better than the F/A-18 system at the time, with the ability to see all radar targets and individually attack them as Targets of Opportunity. We had the ability to guide the brand new AGM-84E SLAM [Stand-off Land Attack Missile] carried by the A-6E, new RHAW missile warning receivers and weapons software that allowed us to drop green [dumb] bombs and canister weapons from high altitude. And, probably best of all, we had received the AN/ALQ-165 ASPJ [airborne self-protection jammer], which was never operationally approved, but was much better than the Vietnam-era AN/ALQ-126 previously fitted to the A-7. The bottom line was our trusty "Harleys" [nickname given to the Corsair II] were as high tech as any of the other aircraft in the fight. We were feeling pretty good and our bomb hits from high altitude (15,000 ft release) were also pretty good.

'Around the beginning of October, it looked like we may really have to fight Iraq. Diplomacy was not going well, the Coalition was forming, and the massive movement of troops, weapons and materiel were all landing in Saudi Arabia. The CAOC [Combined Air Operations Center, located in Riyadh, Saudi Arabia] wanted to test out the Day One air plan. *Saratoga* planned and led the first strike, with Cdr [Michael T] "Spock" Anderson, CO of VFA-81, as strike lead. I had lead of the "JFK" side of the strike, and our scheme was to link up our 22 A-6s, EA-6Bs, F-14s and A-7s with four USAF KC-135s over Saudi Arabia, top off several times and then simulate a drop off just south of Iraq.

'The war plan had the Navy taking the west side of Baghdad, while the Air Force "Wild Weasels" and EF-111s would work the east side. The target was the Iraq KARI (Iraq spelled backward in French) system, which was an integrated air defense system built by France prior to the war. To take it down, we would have to hit the command bunkers, airfields, air defence radar and missile systems. Our plan was to fire continuous HARMs into the Baghdad area while our A-6s and British Tornados attacked Al-Taqaddum air base. EA-6Bs with F-14 escorts would cover us. It was going to be a big effort. We would simulate all of this in Saudi airspace for the practice event.

'It was very fortuitous that we were able to fly the strike a few times prior to execution. Our first attempt was a disaster. The Air Force tankers flew their normal cell of four, with 500-ft stepdown and 60-mile orbits. Great for a four-plane on a cross-country, but with individual A-6s, EA-6Bs

The Naval Aviators of VA-46 pose with the CVW-3's Golden Tailhook plaque towards the end of the 1990-91 deployment. Under the leadership of Cdr Mark Fitzgerald (kneeling second from right), the unit had secured this highly prized accolade for every line period of the cruise thanks to its superior ball flying and boarding rates. VA-46 also had five pilots in the top ten tailhookers for the deployment (*US Navy*)

A-7s from both VA-46 and VA-72 move towards CV-67's catapults for an 0030 hrs launch cycle on 17 January 1991 to signal the start of *Desert Storm* for CVW-3. 'Decoy 400' (BuNo 160552), which would ultimately complete 31 missions, carries three HARMs, while 'Tartan 310' (BuNo 160615), with its pilot, Lt Jeff Greer, has its unique loadout of four TALDs (*US Navy*)

and A-7s rendezvousing comm out at night without air-to-air radar, it quickly became a calamity. About half the aircraft aborted back to the ship and we regrouped. I was sent into Riyadh to talk to the planners in the CAOC "Black Hole". We found a true hero for the Navy there in the form of Brig Gen Patrick P Caruana, head of the tanker cell. He understood our problem and managed to change USAF tanker procedures for the next strikes, and throughout the war. The tankers flew a 15-mile orbit with 1000-ft vertical spacing – much more to the Navy liking and much easier and safer for all. I led the next practice strike, as "Sara" had left for a Haifa port call, and on my return "JFK" was now the lead carrier. Things now went much smoother, but there was still plenty to learn.

'As we moved into December, each of the carriers had a chance to get a few port calls in the Med and return to our Red Sea MODLOC [Modified Location]. It was really getting serious now. My XO, Cdr [John R] "JR" Stevenson, had convinced the junior officers that they all needed a personal weapon to carry, as the "38 specials" that were standard issue wouldn't do. There had been a panic buy before we left Florida, and an assortment of 9 mm and 0.357 Magnum handguns were on display in the Ready Room. Several of the pilots looked a lot like "Pancho" Villa as they practiced manning up with this additional firepower.

'We also set about modifying our jets by removing two weapons pylons. This still allowed us to carry a drop tank (which we did for the first few days of the war), but gave us a lot more airspeed and increased the available g. Continual mission practice meant we were really clicking now. Tanking off the KC-135 "Iron Maiden" had become routine, getting an Alpha Strike launch airborne was no problem for the terrific "JFK" deck crew and "OK 3s" [best rating for an arrested landing on a carrier] were the norm. We were ready!

'Christmas and New Year's came and went and we started month five of our "three-month" cruise. We had many visitors to the ship but none more important than Capt Carlos Johnson and his SPEAR [Strike Protection and Anti-Air Warfare Research] Naval Intelligence Command team. We now understood how the KARI system worked and how to dismantle it. The plans were laid and the team was ready.

'On 14 January we got the prepare to execute orders. CAG called the COs into his stateroom and we had a very sobering and comprehensive rundown of what we were getting ready to do. This was real and it was going to be hard. I returned to the ready room and got the XO and Department Heads together. We sorted out how we wanted to run the war for our squadron. The pilots would plan and fly, the maintenance officers and chiefs would run maintenance, and paperwork be damned. More importantly, we wanted a set of guidelines for our pilots that we easily understood and executed. Speed is life, stay above 10,000 ft (later revised to 12,000 ft), go below 10,000 ft only if in direct support of troops in danger, keep the aircraft moving and head on a swivel, section integrity, etc. The next day we had an all officers meeting and a good discussion. As I looked each pilot in the eye, it was clear to me that they knew it was going to be a tough fight but they were ready.'

Aside from the Naval Aviators assigned to VA-46 and VA-72 and now ready to go to war, two former Corsair II pilots held senior positions on board CV-67 during the aircraft's final deployment. The *John F Kennedy* Battlegroup Commander, Rear Admiral Riley Mixson (who would also be in overall charge of Battle Force Yankee/TF-155 in the Red Sea), had led A-7B-equipped VA-215 into combat during the latter stages of the Vietnam War. Capt John Warren, CV-67's Air Boss, was also a veteran Corsair II pilot, and he appreciated having the veteran light attack aircraft on board the carrier during the high tempo operations of *Desert Shield* and *Desert Storm*;

'I really enjoyed watching the A-7s get out there and participate in their last war. It was a pleasure having them on the deck because they were so agile and so consistently up. They were always ready and easier to get to the catapults than larger aircraft. This was very important as the heightened level of daily operations made it hard for the flightdeck crew to maintain the catapults and arresting gear, as well as keep the flightdeck petroleum-free. Without a good non-skid base, the deck became very hazardous. The flightdeck and hangar deck crews quickly became experts on how to manoeuvre aircraft under these conditions, especially during a launch. They kept the planes in a sequence so that we didn't have too many aircraft in the same spot, allowing room for a plane to slide. The pilots also got proficient at knowing when to apply the brakes, as well as how to apply power when needed so they wouldn't slide.'

The aerial campaign to liberate Kuwait, codenamed Operation *Desert Storm*, started in the early hours of 17 January 1991. On the first night aircraft from four carriers were involved – *Saratoga* and *John F Kennedy* from the Red Sea and *Midway* and *Ranger* from the Arabian Gulf. *America* had just reached station but was not included due to tanker constraints, with CVW-1 launching its first strikes on day two. *Theodore Roosevelt* was, meanwhile, moving rapidly around the Arabian Peninsula and would enter the Arabian Gulf on the third day of the campaign.

Compared to the 'drive-by' strikes – Grenada and Lebanon in 1983, Libya in 1986 and *Praying Mantis* in 1988 – that had seen limited involvement by Corsair II units during the previous decade, in *Desert Storm* VA-46 and VA-72 were committed to an intense aerial campaign on a level not seen since Vietnam. The coming operation would prove a test for both squadrons and their veteran jets.

Cdr Mark Fitzgerald would lead the first strike flown by aircraft assigned to Battle Force Yankee/TF-155;

'At 0030 hrs on 17 January, I was the first aircraft off the cat leading the Navy armada north from the Red Sea to our rendezvous with the tankers and on to Baghdad. All the anticipation, the self-doubts, and the adrenaline rush of the previous days seemed to leave on the cat shot. It was time for business, and the training and discipline learned since the first day of flight school was now at work.

'Tartan 312' (BuNo 160717 – the youngest of VA-46's 11 A-7s) has its tanks topped off from a KC-135 over central Saudi Arabia during the early stages of the war. Although seen here armed with 1000-lb Mk 83 bombs, this aircraft had fired three HARMs on Night One of the war when it led the CVW-3 strike on Baghdad with Cdr Mark Fitzgerald at the controls (*US Navy*)

'We rendezvoused with the tankers comm out. We could not break the radar horizon or comm silence until the F-117s and Tomahawks dropped on Baghdad. It was 750 nautical miles from the Red Sea to Baghdad, and mission length was going to be five hours' flying. It took several cycles through the KC-135 to get everyone topped off. At 1000 lbs per minute fuel transfer, and six aircraft on a drogue, each jet had to get in and get out quickly so that all six aircraft were topped off at the drop off point. After four or five tankings for each aircraft, we all had a full bag of gas.

'Coming up on the AWACS control frequency, the chatter had started. Bogies were airborne around Baghdad, our scopes were full of SAM sites that were radiating and the weather was not really great. With 84 Navy, USAF and RAF aircraft all heading to Baghdad, and F-117s egressing, everyone had to be on altitude, time and location.

'As we exited the tankers just south of the Iraqi border and checked in with AWACS, we were notified of a flight of four MiGs airborne west of Baghdad. As we proceeded in, the northernmost F/A-18, flown by Cdr "Spock" Anderson – the *Saratoga* strike lead – called that he was locked on a [MiG-25] "Foxbat". However, due to the strict rules of engagement, he was unable to fire since the AWACS did not have radar contact with the MiG-25. "Spock" continued inbound, breaking lock when the MiG headed west away from Baghdad. "Spock" and his wingman, Lt Cdr Scott Speicher, were each carrying three HARMs to cover the inbound strike of four A-6s and four low-altitude RAF Tornados against Al-Taqaddum air base. Post-war analysis revealed that the MiG circled back east and shot Lt Cdr Speicher down from the rear. The MiG then headed south toward the A-6 strikers. My flightpath was directly between these aircraft.

'The weather was very hazy, and there was an overcast layer at 25,000 ft. This put the F/A-18s above and A-7s below the overcast – we could not see the Hornets. I started getting steady strobes on my radar warning receiver, and my ASPJ went into repeat on the air-to-air radar threat. I expended several rounds of chaff, which seemed to break the lock. I heard the roar of afterburners above my cockpit, which I assumed post-strike was the MiG passing south – he went right through the middle of our formation.

'About 70 miles from Baghdad, the weather broke and the sight was impressive. There was literally a dome of lead over the city, with missiles

popping out the top. Decoys, bombs and Tomahawks had brought every SAM system on line. I quickly turned my attention back to firing two of my pre-briefed HARM. Each HARM-equipped aircraft would fire two missiles from pre-determined launch positions, and the third missile would be fired in Target of Opportunity [TOO] mode against any emitting sites that were left. I fired my first missile – we were all warned not to look at the missile plume, for it would temporarily blind us. Of course I looked, and had stars twinkling in my eyes. For the next missile, I didn't look until it had climbed to its perch at 80,000 ft.

'Now it was getting exciting. The pre-briefed shots could be fired outside missile range, but TOO range was much closer. As the HARM system was new, we did not have a lot of training. My scope had a symbol I had not seen before, a flashing "6" in a blinking box. Fascinated, I studied it a bit too long, only to look up and see an SA-6 SAM pitching over and heading in my direction. I quickly shot my HARM, hit my chaff – which, apparently, was empty from the MiG encounter – and commenced a very hard breaking turn away. I watched my HARM go almost straight down in the direction of what appeared to be the SAM's launch site. A satisfying explosion of a HARM and a disappearing SAM warning light indicated that the missile had done its job.

'As the strike package exited, very few of the radars were still radiating. The SEAD strike had done its job. From this point forward, no integrated SAM defence was ever mounted by Iraq, and only SAM ambush tactics were employed for the rest of the war. We had briefed that if the air war got too intense, get low and get out of country. One of our pilots had seen enough of the MiGs and called egressing low (1000 ft). As we closed on Mudaysis air base in southwestern Iraq, a Crotale SAM site came up and started firing at him – one final piece of excitement.

'We now were all low on fuel, and joined on the tankers to start the refuelling daisy chain again. Each aircraft could only get a few thousand pounds initially so that the next jet could tank – a procedure that led to many exciting low-fuel experiences throughout the war! Back to the ship for a night landing and some really great sea stories.'

A HARM streaks away from 'Decoy 403' (BuNo 157478) during a live fire exercise in the early stages of CVW-3's work-ups in 1990. Pilots were warned not to look at the missile plume when the HARM was fired at night as it would temporarily blind them. When launched in TOO mode the AGM-88A would rapidly climb up to its perch at 80,000 ft prior to then diving on its target (*US Navy*)

Lt John D Klas of VA-46 was one of the eight HARM 'shooters', and he provided the following account for the squadron's Operation *Desert Storm* Combat Diary;

'It was Night One of the war. We didn't know yet we would enjoy air superiority in less than ten days. We also didn't know that the MiGs would later run away from our fighters and flee to Iran.

'As my lead [Cdr D L Donovan] turned his lights out at the border and disappeared into the pitch-black night, I knew it was time for the show. We'd meet Air Force tankers over Saudi Arabia after taking off from *John F Kennedy* in the Red Sea. Fully fuelled, we headed for Baghdad, each on our own mission, hoping to slip through the overlapping Iraqi radar network.

'We listened to the AWACS, our eyes in the sky, for details of Iraqi air activity. "Picture Clear" – that's what we liked to hear. The we heard, "MiG-25 'Foxbat' north of your position". Then I really got tense. The skipper [Cdr Fitzgerald] came across on the radio and said, "Hang in there guys". The MiG came within 40 miles of my position and could have easily run me down, but he never saw me. Maybe he ran low on gas or maybe he saw too many blips on his radarscope. I'll never know. I got to my launch position, shot my missiles at SAM sites around Baghdad and made the turn to head outbound, jinking through AAA and watching SAMs to make sure they weren't tracking on me. My missile alert light lit up so many times I lost count. On the way back to the border I listened for the MiG but never heard of it again. Forty minutes after my lead's lights went out I was safely south of the border and looking for the tanker again. I was glad to see the ship that night, and after my five-hour flight I bagged an OK 3-wire.

'That night proved a few things. First, the five months of training in the Red Sea and practice missions we flew paid off. Second, our tactics were correct and properly employed, and third, we were ready and able for that strike on Night One.'

Lt Jeff Greer stands by his A-7, 'Tartan 310', the evening prior to flying both his and VA-46's only TALD mission of the campaign. Greer is leaning on one of the ADM-141A decoy missiles he would expend just a few hours later (*US Navy*)

TALD

Not all the Corsair IIs participating in the first night strike of *Desert Storm* were HARM shooters, with two jets (one each from VA-46 and VA-72) undertaking a unique mission aimed at confusing, rather than destroying, the Iraqi air defence system. VA-46's Lt Jeff Greer was flying one of these aircraft;

'The day before Night One of *Desert Storm* was understandably filled with anticipation and trepidation. We had known what our Night One mission would be since August, and had practiced it numerous times. We were ready. I was to be a decoy. It was my job to go in first and drop four [ADM-141A] TALDs (Tactical Air Launched Decoy). The TALD had a square fuselage, and after deployment the wings popped out and it became a highly radar-reflective glider [with a range of up to 70 nautical miles when dropped from high altitude]. The theory was my four TALDs would make me look like a flight of five aircraft. Seeing me coming, the Iraqis would light me up with their radar and start shooting, allowing those behind me to launch HARMs up and over me to take out their radars and give the main strike package a clearer route to Baghdad.

'When the time came to go, I was the third plane launched off *Kennedy*. Planes from both carriers in the Red Sea rendezvoused on the three KC-135 tankers. Having roughly 36 planes coming from different directions and trying to rendezvous on the three tankers at night was just the first step. After I got my fuel, I proceeded alone on my planned mission route. To make it more difficult to be seen at night, we turned off all of our exterior lights and went in alone. Why alone at night? You can't fly formation off a plane you can't see.

'Each time we rehearsed our Night One mission, we went right up to the Iraq border and turned around. On Night One, we continued. My first thought as I crossed the border into Iraq was, "Wow! I just flew into another country without their permission". Shortly after I entered Iraqi airspace, I saw a plane with its lights on at my "twelve o'clock" coming towards me. Knowing that we were supposed to have our lights out, that I was the first in and that this plane was coming *from* Iraq, I mentally prepared for what might happen next. I proceeded on my course and watched the plane as it moved to my "one o'clock" position, then my "two", "three" and "four o'clock". It appeared to be circling to manoeuvre behind me. Then, as it passed my "five o'clock", its lights went out! I remember thinking this might be a short war for me, but as I waited, looked and prepared, nothing happened. I have no idea where he went.

'I proceeded to my pre-briefed launch point and released my TALD, launching them with one press of the button. They came off in rapid succession one at a time so they didn't hit each other. On my way out of Iraq, I saw a good bit of AAA, which fell short of my altitude. Other than that, egress was uneventful. I crossed back into Saudi Arabia, got fuel from one of the KC-135s and returned to trap on board *Kennedy*.

'One mission down, 22 more to go.'

A total of 137 TALDs were expended by the US Navy primarily during the opening three days of the campaign.

FIRST DAY STRIKE

Less than four hours after the Night One strike package had returned to 'JFK', CVW-3 launched its first day missions of *Desert Storm*. The six HARM-equipped A-7Es sortied by VA-46 were led by Lt Cdr Val Diers (who was at the controls of 'Tartan 312', which Cdr Fitzgerald had used in the air wing's opening attack on Baghdad);

'The first day missions by CVW-3 aircraft consisted of dual CV strikes to H-2 and H-3 air bases in western Iraq. Both strike groups included two A-7s equipped with Walleyes that were to be aimed at hangars and fuelling stations at the respective sites. Defenses were extensive, consisting of dense AAA and Roland and SA-6 SAMs.

'My mission was to lead the SEAD support for *Saratoga*'s H-3 strike. My strike group consisted of six A-7s and two A-6s, each carrying three HARMs.

'I had flown with Lts [T H] Aslin, [B H] Mercer and [K H] O'Mara on previous Mirror Image Strikes [during *Desert Shield*], but Lt O'Mara's aircraft had mechanical problems on deck so Lt(jg) "Gerbil" Goebel launched as the spare. This caused an airborne reshuffle of wingmen because I wanted "Gerbil" on my wing – he was the most junior pilot in the squadron. Mercer and Aslin made up the second "Tartan" section.

'We launched, rendezvoused and tanked just as we'd done on five previous practice missions. Off the tankers just southeast of Al-Jouf [in Saudi Arabia], my element was on its own. Updating our systems over Jalibah, an Iraqi border town on "pipeline road", we were in strike formation – four sections in combat spread, with seven to eight nautical miles between sections. Timing was more perfect than on any previous practice mission. Our Corsair IIs were flying at 540 knots. Sidewinders were selected until ten miles from HARM launch. Bogies were capping, running and popping up everywhere. The HARMs were launched with precision. It looked like a rocket barrage because each HARM was launched at the same piece of sky, causing a huge funnel of smoke coursing towards H-3.

'I was taking pictures of HARMs launching and possible ground installations when I looked up to see two jets explode in big dirty fireballs. They were co-altitude and approximately eight to ten nautical miles away at my 1130 position. I had launched my last HARM just prior to the explosions, and after throwing my camera down, all I could do was watch two fireballs crash to earth in two large dark grey explosions. Remorse was a first emotion because I thought they were two of five Hornets that had just passed over my strike group.

'Each section egressed unscathed, and my section was to pump back behind the defenceless A-6s. All HARM shots were from 21,000-24,000 ft. Our pump back towards the target brought my section down to 18,000 ft. We followed the A-6s through their HARM launches and secured their "six" as they exited south. I had briefed a high egress if there was no air opposition and low if MiGs were about – we exited at 100 ft, evading an Iraqi border post in the process. The rest of the mission was uneventful, and we returned without tanking.

'At the debrief we were happy to learn that all strike aircraft had returned, and the two downed jets were Iraqi MiG-21s. Mission No 1 complete.'

One of the Iraqi Air Force (IrAF) aircraft Lt Cdr Diers saw being destroyed was credited to former A-7 pilot Lt Cdr Mark Fox, now flying an F/A-18C with VFA-81 from *Saratoga*. He hit the enemy fighter with Sidewinder and Sparrow missiles, before going on to bomb H-3 air base. The second aircraft was credited to Lt Nick Mongillo, also from VFA-81.

SLAM

Although not carried into combat by the A-7 during *Desert Storm*, the AGM-84E SLAM (acquired as a replacement for the AGM-62 Walleye

II glide bomb) relied on the Corsair II and its AN/ on AWW-9B datalink pod for terminal guidance to the target when A-6E-equipped VA-75 of CVW-3 gave the weapon its operational debut during the evening of 18 January. The unit's Intruders headed a night strike to northwestern Iraq, the primary target being the Haditha dam and its adjacent power plant.

Two A-6Es and two A-7Es from VA-46 split from the main strike force to conduct an attack that saw the first combat use of the

The Al-Qa'im superphosphate plant near Baghdad was targeted by AGM-84E SLAMs fired from A-6Es of VA-75 and guided by an A-7E from VA-46 equipped with an AN/AWW-9B datalink pod during the evening of 18 January 1991. This photograph was taken during the attack, which was the first time the precision stand-off weapon had been used operationally (*US Navy*)

AGM-84E. The Intruders fired one missile each at around 65 nautical miles from the target – the Al-Qa'im superphosphate fertiliser plant involved in the production of so-called 'yellowcake' that can be used in the processing of uranium for weaponising.

The A-7Es guided the missiles – via a video/command guidance datalink to each SLAM – from 85 nautical miles (inbound run) and then 105 nautical miles (outbound run) to/from the target. The first SLAM directly hit the aim point, identified as a building containing uranium extraction laboratories, while the second missile entered through the hole created by the first, as the mission video clearly depicted. Precision guided weapons – embraced by the media as 'smart weapons' – had arrived. A second SLAM strike on the Al-Qa'im facility was aborted on the evening of 24 January due to technical difficulties with the escorting F-14. It was successfully completed a day later, with SLAM video recorded by the AN/AWW-9B pod attached to the A-7E of VA-46's Lt Hank K Gibson confirming a direct hit on a building that was also believed to house uranium extraction laboratories.

Cdr Fitzgerald provided more details of the first SLAM mission;

'We had been analysing the Iraqi nuclear efforts and Coalition intel had discovered a suspicious site [manufacturing superphosphate] near the Syrian border at Al-Qa'im, affectionately called "Big Al". Protected by a SAM and AAA ring, it became a priority target. Just before cruise, each of our A-7 squadrons had sent a pilot to the west coast to learn the SLAM system. The weapon consisted of a Harpoon missile body with GPS navigation and IR homing controlled from a datalink pod.

'On the second night of the war, our pilot, Lt "Hoot" Gibson, was to fly the control aircraft, while two A-6Es from VA-75 sortied with a single SLAM each. The missiles were launched more than 60 nautical miles from the target, and "Hoot" guided them to perfect hits. The video [from the attack] was so good that it became a briefing favourite, and was later turned into a commercial for a major defence contractor.'

'CORSAIR KID'

XO of VA-72, Cdr John 'Lites' Leenhouts (who had accumulated more than 1000 carrier landings by the time he was a lieutenant commander, earning him the nickname 'Corsair Kid'), was also heavily tasked during the opening missions of *Desert Storm*;

'We started from Night One going all the way to the outskirts of Baghdad and the surrounding areas – Samawah, Al-Qa'im, Al Asad, Al Qurnah, Al Khafi, Tallil, H-2 and H-3. We visited all the major air bases and numerous other strategic targets as well. Initially, HARMs were employed, then Walleyes as we went after command centres, bridges and radar sites.

'On 19 January, somewhere around 0200 hrs, I was leading a flight of six A-7Es tasked to provide SEAD for a strike package of six A-6Es that were going after a headquarters building at an airfield west of Baghdad. We were out in front of the EA-6Bs, with the A-6Es following closely. Our A-7Es were loaded with three HARMs apiece, and no external fuel tanks – the planes had been basically cleaned up to reduce drag. Three HARMs was the maximum load carried. You could always expend one, but you didn't want to throw two away. You never wanted to carry more than you had a high probability of using. We would recover with one or two HARM, but not three. Each one equated to about 1000 lbs of fuel. Although you *could* actually recover with three, you had to be really low on fuel, and that wasn't a good idea.

'During *Desert Shield* we had conducted numerous training sorties uploaded with a FLIR pod and a single external tank. However, before hostilities began it was decided to drop wing pylons 3 and 7 – a centre and an inboard pylon – while the opposite inboard pylon was maintained

Armed with an AGM-62B, 'Decoy 402' (BuNo 158819) is Iraq-bound. Both Walleye Is and IIs were expended by VA-46 and VA-72 in *Desert Storm*, this weapon being unique to the A-7 during the campaign. Less than 30 television-guided AGM-62s were used in total, and after the conflict had ended the Walleye I/II was retired from the inventory (*US Navy*)

in case we wanted to carry a tank. The FLIR pod was more weight than it was worth. By dropping it and the two pylon stations, the jet was able to maintain over 525 knots on the deck.

'During the first two nights Iraqi radars were very active. Therefore, pre-briefed [PB] HARM launches were employed. However, by Night Three, they had started "blinking" their radars – they got smarter – so the PB method was no longer practical, thus the TOO mode was the order of the night. I was working at my assigned altitude block of 23,000-24,000 ft. I was slightly off axis, and was coming in at 30-40 degrees off the strike axis – you never wanted to be over the top of the strike aircraft, which in this case were going to conduct a multi-axis attack.

'On this particular night [19 January] we had tail winds upwards of 130-160 knots, and unpredicted. I was setting up my EOB [Electronic Order of Battle] orbit, which is more or less an oval racetrack circuit, while attempting to establish a precise timeline so that we could cover A-6E strikers. They were strung out in a long stream at medium altitude, slightly above 20,000 ft, and we were tasked to cover them while they were within the various SAM engagement rings. I planned to arrive at the forward edge of my assigned threat ring at approximately the same time the strikers were going through this ring and others that overlapped. The SAM sites were to the west of Baghdad, and we were going to be kept quite busy working them as the A-6Es ingressed and then egressed the 30- to 45-mile engagement zone. A lengthy, 15-18 minutes' window of protection was required to cover the site.

'The expectation was that the SAM's tracking, and then acquisition radars would light us up, at which point we would hopefully be provided with an opportunity to pick off the radar sites. When the radar tracking

'Decoy 407' (BuNo 158839) and 'Decoy 400' (BuNo 160552) are both missing at least one pylon, with the aircraft closest to the camera lacking two. The practice of removing pylons to reduce drag and save weight began during the Vietnam War (*US Navy*)

system illuminated your aircraft, that meant they were looking at you and fixing to fire before they got their fire control on you. You had to wait 3-7 seconds, or however long you felt good about, before unleashing a missile – the plan was to unleash the first salvo of HARM at this point. All we were working with [when it came to detecting active target acquisition radar] was the aircraft's AN/ALR-45 RHAWS [Radar-Homing And Warning System]. The HARM's seeker head also provided additional EW [electronic warfare] information. As such, you were somewhat reluctant to get rid of one until you had something locked up.

'As we were hauling the mail to the target, those horrendous winds came into play. I had worked out a precise timeline in my mind to get to the edge of the SAM engagement envelope, but I had not calculated those trailing winds that were now driving me eastward. The end result was that I didn't realise until I got into the heart of the SAM ring that I was in it. I was mentally trying to keep myself out of its lethal envelope, while waiting for the SAMs' tracking radar to light me up. The tactic to be employed was to shoot, then turn out so that I had room to manoeuvre and to give myself the SAM evasion timeline should a launch occur. You needed to be able to observe the initial tell-tale trailing inferno of the missile – this was how you determined if you were the target. If you saw the missile streaking across the sky, it wasn't coming for you, but if you saw what looked like a black dot in the night sky, this usually meant the missile was headed straight for you.

'As I was going in, a SAM site's radar locked me up, so I shot and the HARM headed straight for the radar – which was a good sign. In the TOO mode, the missile headed straight for the radar source, while in the PB mode, it went up and then came back down, seeking out an active radar emitter. Of course, the site's radar was in a "blinking" mode, so I didn't know if the operator knew that I was shooting or not. I'm not sure if my initial missile hit the target, but it was working as advertised and I was happy. I now turned 180 degrees while punching out chaff as I continued on the outbound leg of the racetrack, so now I was flying into the headwinds. Consequently, I was having difficulty getting away, and I was getting a really sick feeling!

'As I continued on the inbound leg of the racetrack, the site was still up. So it was obvious the operator must have shut down soon after my launch. Although a HARM will continue to home in on the location of the radar source even after the emitter is shut down, the missile's accuracy starts degrading rapidly upon shutdown – consequently, it has to be dead-on, or it's not going to do any damage. On this second run in, the site just tickled me, and wouldn't lock me up long enough for me to take a shot. On my way out, I again punched out chaff.

'During the next orbit the site locked me up once again and I was able to squeeze off another HARM, and again this one went straight. By this time, I was certain the operator had figured out that I was shooting at him. When we fired a HARM we were required to broadcast in clear voice the word "Magnum" to alert other Coalition aircraft to the fact that a HARM was in the air. Once the Iraqis worked this out, they started shutting down their radars when they heard it, which sometimes worked to our advantage. Therefore, we started changing code words.

'I was now down to my last missile, but I'd really liked to have saved it so that I could maintain as much situational awareness as possible. Ideally, you always wanted to have at least one HARM onboard during the egress, as it provided you with much better ELINT (electronic intelligence).

'In my cockpit I was trying as best I could to maintain good situational awareness of the threat profile. I knew where the radar emitter was, and I was aligned against its SA-3 – the site never put its SA-6 on me, nor its SA-8 that was known to be in the area. However, an earlier event may have taken the SA-8 down and the Intel may not have reached us. So on my fourth run in, I took it all the way in to about four miles, meaning that I was in the heart of the SAM's envelope. At that moment, I'm certain that the operator thought he had me, as he came up with not only the tracking, but also the fire-control radar as well – we were in business now. Although I didn't witness this, I'm sure he launched and was hoping to track on me, but I let go with my third and final missile.

'Not knowing if in fact a SAM had been launched, I punched out a cloud of chaff and opted to make a diving descent below it. I descended to around 10,000 ft, which was going to break any missile lock – even that close – rather than turn away and be held up by the headwind. A SAM was launched, but never tracked me, so I'm relatively certain that the radar operator most likely shut down yet again at the last second. I'll never know if I killed that site. All I do know is that it didn't get me.

'Now I was down there, and had violated the rule – don't change your altitude – because there are planes out there everywhere. So as best I could, while fighting those headwinds, I made a slow and methodical climb while keeping my speed up, as I knew I couldn't climb very fast. When I was about 14-15 miles from the radar site, I knew I was still in the envelope of the SA-3, but outside the weapon's lethal range.

'While heading back to the boat, a call came from "Bulldog" – the on-scene AWACS – warning that there was activity over Mudaysis air base, southwest of the border. This particular airfield had been utilised regularly as a sort of dumpsite. Everyone seemed to go there to expend any unused ordnance that couldn't be brought back to the boat. The inhabitants had had enough and were getting a little perturbed about this, and now a nearby SA-2 site was going active.

'I had been duelling earlier, and in doing so had expended all of my HARMs. Consequently, my RWR [radar-warning receiver] situational awareness had been degraded somewhat and now I was flying through a

A CNN news team films a pilot from VA-46 as he stows maps and his helmet prior to climbing into 'Tartan 303' (BuNo 160551) for the 20 January 1991 mission against targets surrounding An Najaf air base. Armed with four Mk 83 bombs, this aircraft was launched as the air spare but returned to the carrier when all six primary aircraft from VA-46 pressed on into Iraq (*US Navy*)

hot SA-2 threat ring while still fighting 130-knot headwinds. I thought to myself, "This really sucks!" Well, obviously, I made it, but that third night of the war was the worst night of my life.

'Don't get too close. Don't duel with them. These were "don'ts" that had evolved from the Vietnam War, yet I still ended up deeper in the heart of the threat than expected. This was partly due to the winds and because of the desire to protect the strike group. I could have easily thrown away a perfectly good jet, not to mention my own life, while trying to do the right thing because the lives of fellow aviators were at stake. The goal is to successfully suppress the threat by setting yourself up as the bait and driving right at the source of the radar, making yourself the more lucrative target. And during this strike, as was the desire, the SAMs targeted A-7Es solely.'

As Cdrs Fitzgerald and Leenhouts mentioned in their respective mission accounts, chaff was almost always used by Corsair II pilots when engaging Iraqi targets. VA-46 and VA-72 quickly realised that the supply of this expendable was limited in the jet, resulting in impromptu field modifications being carried out as Cdr Leenhouts recalled;

'In the A-7E we only had two AN/ALE-39 chaff/flare buckets located in the tail section, which accommodated some 60 rounds. We usually didn't carry flares, as they would have highlighted us against the night sky. However, upon returning from our initial strikes, we were all complaining that we didn't have enough chaff. One of the air wing ordnance guys resurrected the idea of simply getting an empty coffee can, filling it with chaff, plugging the open end with an oversized sponge with a piece of wire attached, and then wedging it upside-down into each pylon housing. The wire was then attached to the bomb lug of an uploaded bomb, and when the latter was jettisoned, it would pull out the sponge, thus releasing the chaff. This method was only employed when carrying Mk 83 or Mk 84 general-purpose bombs mounted directly to the parent pylon. As we rolled in from altitude, and upon weapons release, we filled the sky with chaff so the Iraqis couldn't put a fire-control radar on us.

'During a strike mission we always took our EA-6Bs along with us, sometimes to within approximately 20 miles of the target, from where they provided great jamming support. The Iraqis would know that we were in the vicinity due to the EA-6Bs' jamming, but they couldn't get any kind of fire control on us. They wouldn't know if they were the intended targets or if we were just passing by until the bombs started to detonate, after which they'd then have a pretty good idea as to where we were, or at least where to look for us. They could then attempt to pinpoint us as we rolled in from high altitude, and if conditions allowed and they could visually sight us, they'd attempt to employ their radar to range us. It was then that the extra chaff really came into its own.'

As had been the case during the Vietnam War, the A-7 quickly proved to be a valuable SEAD asset at the very start of *Desert Storm*. It would continue to provide HARM support whenever it was required, with Lt Cdr W R 'Bud' Warfield of VA-72 undertaking this highly dangerous role on a number of occasions;

'SEAD missions involved great precision from a flying perspective. You had to have your A-7 in exactly the right point in the sky at the correct distance from the target, and the HARM had to be fired at exactly the

right time. We flew some very precise missions, despite being subjected to 90-knot winds at altitude and jinking to avoid SAMs and AAA – the latter could be dangerously mesmerising.

'A week into the war, we were flying a night SEAD mission for an A-6 strike. I was about 30 miles away from the Al-Qa'im superphosphate plant, which was being hit at the same time by two SLAMs. Al-Qa'im was surrounded by something in the order of 175 AAA guns and three SA-3 and two SA-2 sites. I looked at it from 30 miles and thought, "Boy, I'm glad I'm not down there".

'Three days later, I was on a mission [to H-2 air base] with 16 A-7s all loaded with Mk 83 1000-lb bombs. I didn't know if anyone else had the same feeling about the amount of defences the target had. We briefed with a little trepidation – there would be some lead in the air. And sure enough, there was. By that time, we had beaten down their defences to the point where they never shot a missile or a gun until the first bomb hit. Typically, they didn't know we were there. They were too chicken to turn on the tracking radars of their SAMs and most of their GCI [ground control intercept] radars were jammed up pretty good.

'On this mission, when the first bomb went off, the AAA was pretty heavy. I came off target, and it was my first chance to see flak bursts actually going off above me. I was weaving in and out of the flak bursts, which was probably a dumb thing to do. You should always fly right through the burst of a shell that just went off. We were jinking around and everyone was yelling on the radio. I looked back over my shoulder and saw my Dash 3 and Dash 4 were weaving. Dash 3 was actually bracketed. You could see the flak bursts following behind the plane as he went through the sky. They

Cleared to launch from 'JFK's' bow catapult one, 'Decoy 412' (BuNo 158842) is just moments away from being shot off the carrier. The aircraft is armed with six Mk 20 Rockeye canisters, which proved to be the weapons of choice for both Corsair II units in *Desert Storm*. Indeed, VA-46 dropped 783 of them, with a total weight of 195.75 tons. VA-72's numbers were very similar (*US Navy*)

had him in their sights. He was actually Dash 15 coming off target, and they were mad as hornets down there. No one from our air wing was hit, and it was total elation to see the target go away like that.

'AAA has never got the press SAMs have. Everyone thinks SAMs are magical weapons. The fact is that all the SAMs they shot at us – SA-2s, SA-3s, SA-6s and SA-8s, as well as the non-tactical [shoulder-launched] SA-14 and SA-16 – failed to hit any CVW-3 aircraft. All the tactical SAMs were fired unguided because the Iraqis were afraid of HARMs. I think they got the picture after the first night when we took out the SA-6 sites at H-3 air base.'

With the deckcrew having already broken down the chains holding 'Tartan 307' (BuNo 160713) and 'Decoy 404' (BuNo 159971) to the flightdeck, and with their engines idling, the pilots of both aircraft are ready to taxi – although the maintainer leaning into the cockpit of the VA-46 jet indicates there might be a last-minute problem with that jet. VA-46 fired 74 HARMs between 17 January and 13 February, while VA-72 expended 78 during the same period (*US Navy*)

TANKER SUPPORT

Without a doubt, however, after going through all the enemy flak and SAMs, what seemed to be of most concern for the A-7 pilots was refuelling in a sky crowded with other aircraft clustering around USAF KC-135 tankers, whose short-coupled basket-hose arrangements were, at best, ad hoc affairs to accommodate the various naval aircraft they now had to service. The diverging philosophies of the US Navy and USAF has allowed the design of the refuelling equipment to develop into a receiver-driver process in the US Navy, while it is the boom operator in the USAF tanker that guides the refuelling cycle.

Thus, the make-do, unstable basket wobbling behind the large Stratotanker or KC-10 has never inspired confidence in US Navy and US Marine Corps crews. However, when a pilot is down to his last 1000 lbs of fuel, the availability of a tanker is infinitely more important than its size or system.

Cdr Leenhouts explained further;

'A night tanker rendezvous was, without a doubt, petrifying. Day refuelling, however, was fine. It was almost like an ACM [air combat manoeuvring] engagement where everyone was going for the same piece of sky at the same time. We avoided each other, although some of the "belly checks" could surprise you. At night, there was no doubt that if you erred, you put not only your own life in jeopardy but those of dozens of others.

'Once you were on the tanker, just staying there – in some cases while going through difficult weather – demanded that you just suck it up, tighten up until you couldn't see anyone behind you, and focus on the guy in front of you and maybe the two in front of him. If you relaxed and got out of line, the "snake" would start whipping and the tail-end guy would take a beating.

'The way the planes were stacked up, you couldn't vary your altitude. When you ran in-country, if you got off your altitude over Iraq, you had the potential of running into someone else, since we were all flying around with our lights out – 200-300 planes all within a 45-50-mile area. You just couldn't violate good airmanship in this arena.'

VA-72's Lt Cdr Warfield added his impressions of aerial refuelling during the war;

'I think one of the most important training issues was that we hadn't worked with the Air Force during the work-ups. We saw this big flail coming, and we were working some pretty intense fuel figures trying to ascertain how we could get in-country using organic tanking. As soon as we got situated, we started seeing the Air Force tasking orders telling us to meet Air Force tankers. Probably the most significant thing we did to ensure success during the first few days was to fly the "mirror image" strikes. We'd load up 45 planes with iron bombs, meet the KC-135 tankers and do the real, live tanking.

'The first day of the war we joined up our strike with the Eighth Air Force KC-135s – 60 planes all joined up. We flew to Iraq without one word on the radio. We had had a chance to get to know the [USAF] people from Jeddah air base [in Saudi Arabia] when they came out to the ship. It was like a big vacation for them.'

Like other American pilots, Lt J T Young of VA-72 also sampled refuelling from British aircraft;

'Tanking went smoothly because we had practiced refuelling from different types of planes. One night, we had a mission that wasn't as large as a regular strike – it was a SEAD escort for an RAF strike group. We showed up on the tanker and it was a VC10 – something I had never tanked off before. It was another interesting experience. They had the same drogue-and-hose system we used, but with a little more outboard station and with more wing vortices messing with your plane. I found it just as easy to work with the RAF as it was our own crews.'

Five (of six) A-7s from VA-72 formate off a KC-135E while it refuels a tanker-configured A-6E from VA-75 in tanker track 'Raisin' on 20 February 1991. Once the Corsair IIs had also topped off their tanks, they would fly north into Iraq to attack H-2 air base. VA-46 also participated in this mission, with eight of its aircraft being involved. Mk 83 1000-lb bombs were used by both squadrons to destroy 'a pumping station, support facilities and dispersed, revetted aircraft' according to VA-46's Operation *Desert Storm* Combat Diary (*US Navy*)

FINAL BARRICADE

Thanks to the A-7's outstanding reliability, VA-46 and VA-72 managed to twice launch 19 of their combined force of 20 jets during the first few days of *Desert Storm*, drawing praise from Rear Admiral Mixson. From 24 January 1991, however, there were only 19 Corsair IIs available to CVW-3 following a landing incident involving VA-72 A-7E BuNo 157478.

As the aircraft had accelerated down the catapult to signal the start of a mission to attack a lightly defended facility in western Iraq, Lt Tom Dostie felt his aircraft wobble. Something was not right. Once airborne, he started checking things out. An observer on the flightdeck said it looked like he had blown a tyre. Checking his instruments, Dostie saw his No 2 hydraulic pressure rapidly declining, but the engine sounded alright. Nevertheless, he kept his landing gear down. As the spare A-7 launched to take his place, he had another pilot check the jet. 'Looks like the nose gear is trailing', the second A-7 pilot reported.

As he reached the designated area, Dostie punched the salvo jettison button and dropped three Mk 83 1000-lb bombs from stations 1, 2 and 8. The weapon on station 6, right above the AIM-9 on station 5, remained where it was. With the jet's gear down and locked, an interlocker prevented ordnance from jettisoning from the inboard weapons stations for fear of them hitting the extended undercarriage.

Dostie then spent a considerable period of time orbiting the carrier and discussing his predicament with deck personnel on the ship and other Naval Aviators in the air while the A-7's fuel load burned down to lighten the aircraft to a safe landing weight. Maintaining an airspeed of 200 knots, Dostie prepared for a low approach so observers on 'JFK' could examine his A-7. Another Corsair II pilot was sent to make a second visual inspection. As he approached the crippled A-7, he called, 'Oh, man! There's no way you're gonna trap this one!' He had seen the nose gear was down and locked, but it had only one wheel! The axle had broken during the catapult shot and a wheel was gone, while the second was barely hanging on. 'Beauty!' was all Dostie could manage in acknowledgement.

The decision was made to barricade the A-7, and senior officers on board the carrier each gave the oncoming lieutenant a word of encouragement before leaving him to make his approach and, hopefully, his trap.

Setting up for a six-mile straight-in approach, he closed on CV-67. At four miles, the low-fuel master-caution light lit up. Dostie was a little below glide-slope, but otherwise in a good position. He realised the glide-slope setting was off by 0.5 degrees and corrected. Making minor adjustments close-in, the hard-pressed pilot concentrated on getting his aircraft over the deck. At 1436 hrs, his tailhook snagged the targeted 1-wire and the jet

Lt Tom Dostie's 'Decoy 403' (BuNo BuNo 157478) comes to a halt after its barricade arrestment on 24 January 1991. The aircraft's nose gear axle had broken during the catapult shot and a wheel had been lost, while the second one was barely hanging on – it can be seen here bouncing off to the right of the photograph. Forty-eight hours later, after it had been stripped of any valuable parts that could be used to keep other A-7s flying, the Corsair II was buried at sea with full military honours (US Navy)

slipped past the remaining three cables to push through the nylon barricade and then come to a halt.

Ordinarily, the aircraft would have been repaired, but as this was its last cruise BuNo 157478 was struck below to the hangar bay, its flying days over. Forty-eight hours later, after it had been stripped of any valuable parts that could be used to keep other A-7s flying, the Corsair II was buried at sea with full military honours. Although it had slid off *John F Kennedy's* elevator No 4 without any resistance, BuNo 157478 refused to sink beneath the waves until it had been strafed by air wing jets.

FINAL MISSIONS

As the war progressed, the A-7s went into 'bomb truck' mode and flew CAS in Kuwait for Coalition ground forces, while continuing to undertake Alpha strikes into Baghdad and western Iraq when required. Targets became increasingly scarce as the campaign progressed, with the IrAF either flying its surviving aircraft to neighbouring Iran or simply burying them in the desert. When the ground assault began on 24 February, both Corsair II units were tasked with bombing all manner of targets in 'kill boxes' in Kuwait and southern Iraq in direct support of the offensive.

The high mission tempo synonymous with *Desert Storm* was maintained by CVW-3 and its two A-7 units through to the end of the war. Cdr Leenhouts remained in the vanguard of the operation, and he would find himself attacking certain targets on multiple occasions while tallying 24 missions between 17 January and 27 February 1991;

'During the final days of hostilities, I made another – although somewhat unplanned – after-dark visit to H-2 air base in western Iraq. Due to its

An ordnanceman from VA-72 fits an arming wire to the fuse of a Mk 82 500-lb bomb, while in the background others lift an AIM-9L up to the aircraft's fuselage station 4 cheek mount. Mk 82s really came into their own once CVW-3 started flying CAS missions in support of the land campaign to rid Kuwait of Iraqi troops (*US Navy*)

significance, I had been there on Night One of the war. During tonight's visit [on 26 February], 14 aircraft – 12 A-7Es and a pair of A-6Es – were dropping by to finish some MiGs off that had been detected by satellite imagery parked in open revetments. The weapons of choice for the mission were Mk 20 Rockeyes and Mk 82 LDGPs. I was the flight lead, and the plan called for me to lay down a string of eight two million-candlepower LUU-2B parachute-retarded flares to shed some light on the target.

'The weather was clear and there was a full moon, hence the airfield was clearly visible and we were able to acquire our aim points from far out. I figured the flares wouldn't be required. Upon voicing that suggestion to the strike group, the skipper of VA-46, who happened to be flying with us that night, replied that since we've got them, let's go ahead and use them. He then added that the flares should make the task that much easier, thus allowing the group to achieve some good hits. I dropped down from 25,000 ft to 10,000 ft to execute the run, popping a flare every 15 to 20 seconds in a zigzag pattern. After the last flare had been dispensed, the plan of attack called for pairs to roll in in trail at 30-second intervals. I was to climb back up to 25,000 ft, rejoin the group and be the last one in.

'No sooner had the last flare come off, and the first pair of aircraft rolled in, when this target unexpectedly came alive – and this was a place that had been pounded numerous times since *Desert Storm* kicked off. The air defences were unbelievable. There was a steady barrage of AAA fire coming out of there, in addition to some rocket-assisted artillery that was reaching altitudes of 22,000-23,000 ft. And there were also lots of SAMs, albeit unguided. As I was climbing up, the group was rolling in. In the hail of fire, panic set in and I was screaming over the radio in an effort to make sure we were deconflicted as I made my way towards the back end of the formation. I couldn't see the other jets and needed to know where everybody was. Upon joining up at the rear of the formation, I rolled in,

Flying towards Cecil Field on 27 March 1991 after departing CV-67, VA-72's 'CAG bird' stands out in its unique 'Desert Storm' camouflage scheme of brown-and-tan pigment dry paint. The aircraft was meticulously resprayed by the unit's maintenance personnel on the eve of the VA-72's departure from 'JFK'. This photograph, like most of the other air-to-air views of the A-7s during *Desert Shield/ Desert Storm*, was taken by 'Mr Corsair', Cdr 'Lites' Leenhouts (*US Navy*) selected a AAA site as my aim point and delivered my Rockeyes – each one containing a couple of hundred armour-piercing bomblets that put the site to sleep. We finished off the MiGs, and inflicted additional damage to the airfield.

'Ironically, on this night H-2 was our secondary target. It was supposedly thought to be a "milk run", and as such we were probably somewhat at ease – maybe too much so. Due to limited visibility in northern Kuwait, our primary target, which would later be known as "the Highway of Death", was

VA-46's 'Tartan 301' swapped its TPS scheme for retro colours not seen on a squadron aircraft since the early 1980s. The jet was resprayed just prior to the unit fly-off, and after being struck from the inventory on 11 June 1991 it was allocated for preservation within the now-titled National Naval Aviation Museum at NAS Pensacola (*US Navy*)

weathered out. Consequently, we were looking for work, and the JFACC [Joint Force Air Component Commander] sent us to H-2 instead. We knew that the MiGs were there and figured that since this place had been pounded repeatedly since Night One, it would be a relatively low-threat target. We were dead wrong. They were going full-out as if it was Night One. It turned out to be one of the highest threats I'd encountered during the entire war [Cdr Leenhouts' SEAD force had already fired 21 HARMs on Night One, silencing SA-6, SA-8 and Roland SAM batteries defending H-2].'

The last A-7 mission of *Desert Storm* during which ordnance was expended took place in the early hours of 27 February 1991, and it saw six aircraft from both VA-46 and VA-72 search for and destroy troop convoys fleeing along the road between Samawah, 175 miles southeast of Baghdad, and Al Diwaniyah in southern Iraq. Airborne for five hours, pilots used LUU-2B flares to illuminate targets for 44 Mk 82 LDGPs. According to VA-46's Operation *Desert Storm* Combat Diary, 'Strike flexed to Zone T10 for weather, [where] all ordnance [was] expended on AAA sites, vehicles in the open and camouflaged structures, with unknown results due to poor weather. One-way distance [to the target] was 660 miles and recovery was at 0430 hrs'. With Kuwait now liberated, peace was declared the following day.

For 42 consecutive days from 0100 hrs on 17 January, VA-46 and VA-72 had flown 717 sorties totalling more than 3100 hours. While carrying out the SEAD mission, the units had fired 152 HARMs between them (78 for VA-46 and 74 for VA-72). Overall, the A-7 squadrons had expended in excess of 1,000,000 lbs of ordnance during *Desert Storm*. CVW-3 flew off *John F Kennedy* on 27 March 1991 and VA-46 and VA-72 returned home to NAS Cecil Field, thus bringing to an end the final operational deployment of the Corsair II in US Navy service. On 23 May, VA-46 and VA-72 formally said goodbye to the A-7 – a type the units had flown since 1970. Both squadrons were disestablished on 30 June.

'Home is the aviator, home from the sea'. Cdr John 'Lites' Leenhouts is greeted by the children of several friends on the ramp at Cecil Field, his aircraft (BuNo 158819) sporting an impressive scoreboard below the cockpit. Each camel represents a mission that was flown by that specific aircraft during *Desert Storm*, while the weapons represented those dropped from that jet. The total combat missions flown by the individual pilot are indicated under their name on the side of the aircraft (*US Navy*)

APPENDICES

A-7 CORSAIR II SQUADRONS 1975-91

NAVAL AIR FORCES, US ATLANTIC FLEET (AIRLANT)

LIGHT ATTACK WING ONE (LATWINGONE) – NAS Cecil Field, Florida

Designation and Nickname	Type	Carrier Air Wings assigned/Notes
VA-12 'Flying Ubangis'/'Clinchers' from 1982	A-7E	CVW-7, disestablished on 1/10/86
VA-15 'Valions'	A-7B/E	CVW-6, CVW-3, MAG-12, re-designated VFA-15 on 1/10/86
VA-37 'Bulls'	A-7E	CVW-3, CVW-15, MAG-12, CVW-6, re-designated VFA-37 on 28/11/90
VA-46 'Clansmen'	A-7B/E	CVW-1, CVW-7, CVW-3, disestablished on 30/6/91
VA-66 'Waldos'	A-7E	CVW-7, disestablished on 1/10/86
VA-66 'Waldos' Detachment*	A-7E	CVW-3, disestablished on 31/3/87
VA-72 'Blue Hawks'	A-7B/E	CVW-1, CVW-7, CVW-3, disestablished on 30/6/91
VA-81 'Sunliners'	A-7E	CVW-17, re-designated VFA-81 on 4/2/88
VA-82 'Marauders'	A-7E	CVW-8, re-designated VFA-82 on 13/7/87
VA-83 'Rampagers'	A-7E	CVW-17, re-designated VFA-83 on 3/3/88
VA-86 'Sidewinders'	A-7E	CVW-8, re-designated VFA-86 on 15/7/87
VA-87 'Golden Warriors'	A-7B/E	CVW-6, re-designated VFA-87 on 1/5/86
VA-105 'Gunslingers'	A-7E	CVW-3, CVW-15, MAG-12, CVW-6, re-designated VFA-105 on 17/12/90
VA-174 'Hell Razors'	A-7B/C/E and TA-7C	Fleet Replacement Squadron, disestablished on 30/6/88

* Deployed 18/8/86 to 2/3/87 with CVW-3.

NAVAL AIR FORCES, US PACIFIC FLEET (AIRPAC)

LIGHT ATTACK WING, US PACIFIC FLEET (LATWINGPAC) – NAS Lemoore, California

Designation and Nickname	Type	Air Wings assigned/Notes
VA-22 'Fighting Redcocks'	A-7E	CVW-15, CVW-11, re-designated VFA-22 on 4/5/90
VA-25 'Fist of the Fleet'	A-7E	CVW-2, re-designated VFA-25 on 1/7/83
VA-27 'Royal Maces'/'Chargers'	A-7E	CVW-14, CVW-15, re-designated VFA-27 on 24/1/91
VA-56 'Champions'*	A-7A/E	CVW-5, LATWINGPAC from 5/86, disestablished on 31/8/86
VA-93 'Blue Blazers'/'Ravens' from 1976*	A-7A/E	CVW-5, LATWINGPAC from 5/86, disestablished on 31/8/86
VA-94 'Mighty Shrikes'	A-7E	CVW-15, CVW-11, re-designated VFA-94 on 4/5/90
VA-97 'Warhawks'	A-7E	CVW-14, CVW-15, re-designated VFA-97 on 21/1/91
VA-113 'Stingers'	A-7E	CVW-2, re-designated VFA-113 on 25/3/83
VA-122 'Flying Eagles'	A-7B/C/E and TA-7C	Fleet Replacement Squadron, disestablished on 31/5/91
VA-125 'Rough Raiders'**	A-7B/C	Fleet Replacement Squadron, disestablished on 1/10/77
VA-146 'Blue Diamonds'	A-7E	CVW-9, CVW-2, CVW-9, re-designated VFA-146 on 21/7/89
VA-147 'Argonauts'	A-7E	CVW-9, CVW-2, CVW-9, re-designated VFA-147 on 20/7/89
VA-153 'Blue Tail Flies'	A-7B	CVW-19, disestablished on 30/9/77
VA-155 'Silver Fox'	A-7B	CVW-19, disestablished on 30/9/77
VA-192 'Golden Dragons'	A-7E	CVW-11, CVW-9, MAG-12, re-designated VFA-192 on 10/1/86
VA-195 'Dambusters'	A-7E	CVW-11, CVW-9, re-designated VFA-195 on 1/4/85
VA-215 'Barn Owls'	A-7B	CVW-19, disestablished on 30/9/77

* Part of Forward Deployed Naval Forces, Japan, based at NAF Atsugi.

** Fighter Attack Squadron (VFA) 125 'Rough Raiders' was established on 13 November 1980 in preparation to become the F/A-18 Hornet fleet replacement squadron. To maintain aircrew currency, a number of A-7E airframes were allocated to the unit in 1981 and flown until sufficient F/A-18s had been delivered. Note also that the VFA designation's meaning was changed to Strike Fighter Squadron on 25 March 1983.

US NAVAL RESERVE

CVWR-20

VA-203 'Blue Dolphins'	A-7A/B/E	based at NAS Jacksonville, Florida, before relocating to NAS Cecil Field, Florida, on 1/12/77, re-designated VFA-203 on 1/10/89
VA-204 'River Rattlers'	A-7B/E	based at NAS New Orleans, Louisiana, re-designated VFA-204 on 1/5/91
VA-205 'Green Falcons'	A-7B/E	based at NAS Atlanta, Georgia, switched to A-6E/KA-6D from 8/90

CVWR-30

VA-303 'Golden Hawks'	A-7A/B	based at NAS Alameda, California, re-designated VFA-303 on 1/1/84
VA-304 'Firebirds'	A-7A/B/E	based at NAS Alameda, California, switched to A-6E/KA-6D from 7/88
VA-305 'Lobos'	A-7A/B	based at NAS Point Mugu, California, re-designated VFA-305 on 1/1/87

COLOUR PLATES

1

A-7E BuNo 158005/NL 311 of VA-22, USS *Coral Sea* (CVA-43), 15 May 1975

Accepted into service on 25 January 1971, this aircraft initially served with VA-122 the following month before passing to VA-146 in April of that same year. It was issued to VA-22 on 16 June 1972, and went on to serve with VA-25, VA-97, VA-146, VA-304, VA-204 and VA-205 before being retired to the Aerospace Maintenance and Regeneration Center (AMARC) at Davis-Monthan AFB, in Arizona, on 17 June 1988. It was scrapped in November 2008. The aircraft is depicted here in artwork as it appeared on 15 May 1975 when BuNo 158005, flown by Lt(jg) Mark Sloat, participated in the attack on Ream Field, in Cambodia, during the *Mayaguez* Incident. The A-7 carried six Mk 82 500-lb bombs in total, split evenly between outboard wing stations 1 and 8 and one Mk 20 Rockeye canister on stations 2 and 7. The aircraft also carried 1000 rounds for its M61A1 Vulcan rotary cannon installed in the lower port forward fuselage.

2

A-7E BuNo 157444/NL 403 of VA-94, USS *Coral Sea* (CVA-43), 15 May 1975

This A-7E was delivered to the US Navy on 13 April 1970 and issued to VA-113 nine days later, although it was soon passed to VA-27. After service with VA-94, the aircraft moved from Lemoore to Cecil Field in May 1976. Serving initially with VA-12, it was subsequently assigned to VA-15, VA-174, VA-83 and VA-81, before returning to VA-174 in 1986. From here it was sent to AMARC for storage on 15 September 1987. After almost 20 years in Arizona, the A-7 was scrapped in October 2005. The aircraft is depicted in artwork with the same weapons loadout as seen on the VA-22 jet in Profile 1.

3

A-7A BuNo 153241/NF 401 of VA-56, USS *Midway* (CV-41), August 1976

Accepted into service on 28 September 1967, BuNo 153241 reached the fleet when it was issued to VA-147 shortly thereafter and went on to see action when the unit gave the Corsair II its combat debut from *Ranger* later that same year. It also served with VA-125 and VA-153 before being assigned to VA-56 on 12 April 1973. The A-7 was sent to the Military Aircraft Storage and Disposition Center (MASDC) at Davis-Monthan AFB, in Arizona, for storage on 8 August 1977. Six years later it was allocated as a spares source for the Foreign Military Sale of A-7s to Portugal, heading to LTV's Dallas, Texas, factory in October 1983. Eventually discarded, the aircraft was put up for disposal and currently awaits restoration with the Pacific Coast Air Museum in Santa Rosa, California. The jet is depicted here in the markings it wore during the Korean tree trimming incident, when *Midway* and CVW-5 were hastily sent from Japan to patrol off the Korean Peninsula. It is armed with three Mk 83 1000-lb bombs on each of the TERs on stations 2 and 7. Note that the carrier designation CVA, where the 'A' indicated 'Attack', changed to CV on 1 July 1975 to indicate the embarked air wing's more multipurpose role, combining air, surface and antisubmarine missions, depending on what aircraft were involved.

4

A-7A BuNo 153208/NF 302 of VA-93, USS *Midway* (CV-41), August 1976

The aircraft entered the US Navy inventory on 19 May 1967, and commenced service with the Naval Air Test Center's weapons test fleet on 20 December that year. It went on to serve with VA-122, VA-82, VA-174 and the Naval Weapons Evaluation Facility at Kirtland AFB, New Mexico, before being placed in storage at MASDC from 23 December 1970. The aircraft returned to service in 1972, and was eventually allocated to VA-93 on 2 April 1973. Retired once again to MASDC on 26 May 1977, the aircraft was selected in for conversion to A-7P specification for the Portuguese Air Force, with whom it was serialled 5536 (later 15536). After its withdrawal from service, the Corsair II was stored at Alverca Air Base before being scrapped. Its cockpit section was saved, however, and acquired by a private collector in Azeitão, Portugal. This artwork depiction shows the A-7A carrying three Mk 20 Rockeye canisters on TERs on stations 8 (starboard wing) and 1 (port wing), and two 300-gal fuel tanks on stations 6 (starboard wing) and 3 (port wing).

5

A-7E BuNo 158677/NL 306 of VA-22, USS *Kitty Hawk* (CV-63), 1979-80

Accepted by the US Navy on October 18, 1972, this aircraft reached VA-22 two days later. Its career included time with VA-94, VA-195 and VA-146, before receipt by VA-22 once again on 23 January 1985. It then went on to serve with VA-94, VA-195, VA-146 and, for a third time, VA-22. The Corsair II was stricken from the Naval inventory in November 1988. Depicted here during CV-63's 1979-80 WestPac, which saw the carrier spending a brief time in the Indian Ocean during the early stages of the Iran hostage crisis, the aircraft is carrying a buddy refuelling tank, with two 300-gal tanks on stations 7 and 8 on the starboard side. No other stores are carried.

6

A-7E BuNo 157524/NL 402 of VA-94, USS *Kitty Hawk* (CV 63), 1979-80

LTV delivered this A-7E to the US Navy on 17 August 1970, and it initially served with VA-192. BuNo 157524 went on to fly with VA-97, VA-94 and VA-146, before returning to VA-94 on 6 June 1979. By the end of 1980 the aircraft was again operating with VA-146, and it then served with VA-147 and VA-27, before reaching VA-122 in March 1983. It was lost on 6 May 1986 following a mid-air collision with another VA-122 A-7E (BuNo 160727) off the California coast – both pilots were killed. The Corsair II carries two Mk 83 1000-lb bombs on stations 1 and 8, as well as two 300-gal drop tanks on stations 3 and 6.

7

A-7E BuNo 157456/AJ 305 of VA-82, USS *Nimitz* (CVN-68), 1980

Delivered to the US Navy on 28 April 1970, BuNo 157456 joined VA-174 three days later. It went on to serve with VA-37, Naval Air Test Center Patuxent River, in Maryland, and VA-174 once again, before joining VA-82 on 15 November 1977. The aircraft was written off when it suffered Class 'A' damage following a ramp strike aboard

Nimitz on 2 March 1981 as the ship and CVW-8 worked up for another deployment. The jet is depicted here storeless, bar AIM-9L Sidewinders on cheek stations 4 and 5.

8
A-7E BuNo 159308/AJ 403 of VA-86, USS *Nimitz* (CVN-68), 1980

Accepted by the US Navy on 16 December 1974, this Corsair II was assigned to VA-86 two days later and duly remained with the squadron until January 1982. It then went on to serve with VA-12, VA-83, VA-46, VA-66, VA-105, VA-174, VA-203 and VA-72, before being placed in storage at AMARC on 17 April 1990. This aircraft was finally scrapped in spring 2018. Stores depicted here include one Mk 20 Rockeye canister on station 2, one 300-gal tank on station 7 and one AIM-9L Sidewinder each on cheek stations 4 and 5.

9
A-7E BuNo 158834/NK 411 of VA-27, USS *Coral Sea* (CV-43), 1980

Delivered to the US Navy on 21 August 1973, this aircraft joined VA-25 the following day and stayed with the unit until transferring to VA-27 on 12 February 1979. As denoted by the black-and-red bands seen on its right wing, the aircraft participated in CVW-14's 1979-80 WestPac cruise that saw CV-43 spend many weeks in the Indian Ocean during the Iran hostage crisis. It was next assigned to NAF Atsugi-based VA-56 in May 1980 when a number of A-7Es were exchanged between CVW-14 and CVW-5 squadrons at NAS Cubi Point in the Philippines – a common practice as airframes were cycled back to CONUS (Continental US) for depot-level maintenance. The jet's time with VA-56 would be short-lived, however, for it was lost in a fatal crash on 14 November that same year during a bombing training mission from *Midway*.

10
A-7E BuNo 156872/NK 300 of VA-97, USS *Coral Sea* (CV-43), 1980

Accepted into service on 28 February 1970 by VA-25, this A-7E subsequently flew with VA-97 until transferred to VX-5 at Naval Weapons Center (NWC) China Lake, in California, in September 1981. It returned to flying with the US Naval Reserve, first with VA-203 in August 1983 and then VA-205 in July 1984, before being retired to AMARC on 24 June 1988 and scrapped in 2005. Aside from the aircraft's Iran hostage rescue operation identification bands, the A-7 also boasts a colourful rudder because it was VA-97's 'CAG bird'. This normally meant that the aircraft displayed all the colours of the squadrons in the air wing on its tail, usually on the rudder (as depicted here) or over the entire tail surface, and with the so-called 'double nuts' 00 in the modex below the cockpit and on the fin tip. This aircraft is only carrying AIM-9L Sidewinders on cheek stations 4 and 5 and two 300-gal fuel tanks on stations 2 and 7.

11
A-7E BuNo 159294/AE 302 of VA-15, USS *Independence* (CV-62), 1983-84

This A-7E joined the US Navy, and VA-83, on 27 September 1974. Five years later, it moved to VA-37, followed by brief service with VA-174 before joining VA-15 on 17 May 1982. Having completed CVW-6's highly eventful 1983-84 deployment, it moved to VA-86 in August 1984 and then went on to serve with VA-15, VA-174, VA-37

and VA-105. Sent to AMARC in January 1991, the jet was scrapped in October 2011. Depicted here during Operation *Urgent Fury* over Grenada, this A-7 is carrying an aerial refuelling buddy store on station 8.

12
A-7E BuNo 156807/AE 401 of VA-87, USS *Independence* (CV-62), 1983-84

LTV handed over this A-7E on 6 November 1969, the aircraft being passed the next day to VA-147. It went on to serve with VA-25, before delivery to VA-87 on 25 February 1981. Moving to VA-174 in August 1984, the jet subsequently spent more time in the colours of VA-87, followed by VA-86 and VA-83, prior to being placed in AMARC storage on 19 February 1987. It left AMARC by road in March 2005 to become a target on the NAS Fallon, Nevada, range complex. Involved in operations over Grenada, the aircraft is depicted here in a typical armament configuration for Operation *Urgent Fury* – one CBU-59 APAM (note the black thunderbolt marking on the canister to differentiate it from the earlier Mk 20 Rockeye) on stations 1 and 8 and Mk 83 1000-lb bombs on stations 2 and 7.

13
A-7E BuNo 157468/AE 305 of VA-15, USS *Independence* (CV-62), 1983

This A-7 was delivered to the US Navy on 28 May 1970, and VA-81 took it on charge the next day at NAS Cecil Field. It served with VA-174, VA-12 and VA-174 for a second period, before being assigned to VA-15 from 28 October 1981. This was the aircraft that Cdr Edward K Andrews, Commander, CVW-6, was flying when he was shot down during the raid on Syrian positions on 4 December 1983. The stores it carried on the Lebanon raid consisted of three CBU-59 APAM canisters on a TER on station 1, a 300-gal drop tank on station 3, an AIM-9L Sidewinder on station 4, a FLIR pod on station 6 (no Sidewinder on station 5) and three APAMs on a TER on station 8.

14
A-7E BuNo 157566/AE 414 of VA-87, USS *Independence* (CV-62), 1983-84

Delivered to the US Navy on 11 November 1970, this aircraft flew with VA-66 and VA-174 before joining VA-87 on 15 April 1983. It went on to serve with VA-37, VA-81 and VA-174 yet again, before entering AMARC on 26 August 1987. The jet was scrapped in November 2008. BuNo 157566 is shown carrying three Mk 82 500-lb bombs on a TER on station 1, one Mk 82 mounted directly on its pylon on station 2 and a 300-gal drop tank on station 3. It would have carried the same load on the starboard side.

15
A-7E BuNo 157587/AG 405 of VA-12, USS *Dwight D Eisenhower* (CVN-69), 1983

This aircraft was accepted by the US Navy at LTV Dallas on 18 December 1970 and sent to VA-174 at Cecil Field the next day. On 3 October 1972 it was transferred to VA-66, and served with that squadron until reverting back to VA-174 in April 1980. The custody change was because VA-66 had to leave two airframes behind at Cecil for its cruise in *Eisenhower*. BuNo 157587 rejoined VA-66 in March 1981 and was allocated to VA-12 on 15 December 1982, remaining with that squadron until retirement to AMARC on 28 August 1986. It was scrapped in November 2008. As with the aircraft depicted in Profile 14, BuNo 157587 is shown carrying three Mk 82 500-lb bombs on a TER on station 1, one Mk 82 mounted directly on its pylon on station 2 and a 300-gal drop tank on station 3.

16

A-7E BuNo 159659/AG 310 of VA-66, USS *Dwight D Eisenhower* (CVN-69), 1983

This A-7E joined the US Navy on 24 October 1975 and was allocated to VA-87 exactly one week later. In August 1982 it was transferred to VA-66, flying with the squadron until joining VA-86 at the end of March 1984. The jet's time with the squadron was short-lived, however, as it was lost on 28 August that same year in a non-fatal take-off mishap from the airfield at NS Roosevelt Roads, Puerto Rico. It is depicted here configured for aerial refuelling, with its stores consisting of a buddy store on station 1, no Sidewinders and two fuel tanks on stations 6 and 8.

17

A-7E BuNo 157568/AA 410 of VA-81, USS *Saratoga* (CV-60), 1985-86

Accepted on 28 October 1970 and issued to VA-66 the next day, this aircraft went on to serve with VA-174, VA-105 and VA-12, before transferring to VA-81 on 3 January 1985. Although the jet entered the Naval Air Rework Facility at NAS Jacksonville, Florida, on April 17, 1986 (just days after CVW-17 completed its marathon eight-month Mediterranean cruise on board CV-60), it was eventually stricken. The aircraft is configured here with Mk 20 Rockeye canisters, one each directly mounted on pylons for stations 2 and 3, and one 300-gal drop dank on station 6. It would also be carrying a HARM on station 7.

18

A-7E 160713/AA 305 of VA-83, USS *Saratoga* (CV-60), 1985-86

Joining the US Navy on 5 May 1978, this aircraft was issued to VA-174 the following day and moved to VA-81 two years later. It joined VA-83 on 24 September 1980, before moving to VA-46 in June 1987. The jet would remain with this unit for the rest of its career, seeing combat in Operation *Desert Storm* in 1991. BuNo 160713 entered AMARC for storage on 10 June that same year, still wearing its mission tallies. Loaned to the Pima Air and Space Museum in Arizona for preservation in 1994, it was officially purchased by the organisation four years later and remains there at the time of writing. It is depicted here with a HARM on station 1, 300-gal drop tank on station 3 and AIM-9L Sidewinders on stations 4 and 5. It would also have had a Mk 20 Rockeye canister directly mounted on pylons for stations 6 and 7.

19

A-7E BuNo 158667/AB 305 of VA-46, USS *America* (CV-66), 1986

BuNo 158667 was accepted into the US Navy's inventory on 11 July 1972, serving initially with VX-5 at NWC China Lake. From 1976 it flew with VA-86, then VA-83 and VA-81, before being assigned to VA-46 on 27 July 1983. Transferred to VA-105 in September 1986 following the completion of CVW-1's eventful 1986 Mediterranean deployment, the aircraft had been passed on to VA-86 by November of that same year. The jet was still serving with the unit when it was lost on 24 February 1987 while on a sortie from *Nimitz* in

the Mediterranean. The pilot was rescued. The aircraft is depicted in the configuration used by VA-46 during its SEAD missions in Operations *Prairie Fire* and *El Dorado Canyon*, with a HARM on station 1, a 300-gal drop tank on station 3 and single HARMs on stations 7 and 8.

20

A-7E BuNo 159971/AB 405 of VA-72, USS *America* (CV-66), 1986

This A-7 was delivered to the US Navy on 9 March 1976, and it went straight to the NATC test fleet at NAS Patuxent River. It joined VA-72 in August that year, and later flew with VA-174, VA-37, VA-105, VA-15 and VA-66, prior to joining VA-72 on 17 January 1986. The jet would remain with this unit for the rest of its service career, with VA-72 moving from CVW-1 to CVW-7 on 1 October 1986 and CVW-3 on 1 March 1989. Flying as 'Decoy 404', it completed 24 missions in Operation *Desert Storm*. After retirement that summer, the aircraft served as an instructional airframe at NATTC Memphis, Tennessee, before being acquired for preservation at the Carolinas Aviation Museum in Charlotte, North Carolina, in a scheme and markings representative of its final months of service. During operations off Libya in the early spring of 1986, the aircraft was armed with AIM-9L Sidewinders on both cheek mounts (stations 4 and 5) and Mk 20 Rockeye canisters on pylons on stations 2, 7 and 8. It also carried a 300-gal drop tank on station 3 and a FLIR pod on station 6.

21

A-7E BuNo 158675/NH 303 of VA-22, USS *Enterprise* (CVN-65), 1988

This A-7 was accepted on 26 October 1972 into the US Navy inventory, passing to VA-94 six days later. It went on to fly with VA-146, before joining VA-22 on 6 January 1984. It was, however, loaned to VA-122 between May 1984 and February 1985 when VA-22 cruised with CVW-11 in *Enterprise*. The aircraft flew from CVN-65 during CVW-11's one-day War At Sea (codenamed Operation *Praying Mantis*) against the Islamic Republic of Iran Navy on 18 April 1988. The jet was retired to AMARC on 27 April 1989 and left there by road in May 2005 to become a range target at NAS Fallon.

22

A-7E BuNo 158833/NH 301 of VA-22, USS *Enterprise* (CVN-65), 1988

This aircraft was accepted by the US Navy at LTV's Dallas plant on 22 August 1973 and issued to VA-113 two days later. It went on to serve with VA-97 on three separate occasions, as well as two periods with VA-195, plus service with VA-56 and VA-25, before being issued to VA-22 on 13 June 1985. BuNo 158833 was the second 'Beefsteak 301' to receive this experimental colour scheme, BuNo 160537 having been painted in a similar way in early 1987 – the latter jet was transferred out of the unit in July of that year. BuNo 158833 received this unique camouflage towards the end of CVW-11's 1988 deployment on board CVN-65. A participant in the sinking of the Iranian frigate *Sahand* during *Praying Mantis*, the aircraft had a silhouette of the ship painted in white below the cockpit to denote its success. Retired to AMARC on 16 April 1990 having accumulated 7012 flight hours, it was selected for Foreign Military Sale (FMS) to the Royal Thai Navy and sent by road to NADEP Jacksonville for eventual transfer to Thailand in October 1995. The jet subsequently served with No 104 Sqn at U-Tapao (with the serial 1414), and after its retirement and a period of storage was placed on display in Krabi, Thailand, in 2015.

23
A-7E BuNo 158013/NH 302 of VA-22, USS *Enterprise* (CVN-65), 1987

This A-7E was accepted from LTV on 20 April 1971 and was quickly assigned to VA-147. It flew with VA-94, VA-122, VA-195 and VA-146 prior to reaching VA-22 on 14 March 1985. It too was given a one-off camouflage scheme, which was more suited to overland operations in the Middle East than the trio of blue/greys seen on 'Beefsteak 301'. The aircraft would never actually deploy operationally with VA-22, and thus put the 'desert camouflage' scheme to the ultimate test, having left the squadron on 20 May 1987 for service with VA-97. Its replacement would remain in the standard Tactical Paint Scheme. BuNo 158013 flew with VA-97 until 28 November 1989, when it was retired to AMARC. It left here in April 2008, bound for MCAS Cherry Point, North Carolina, for eventual use as a range target.

24
A-7E BuNo 159272/NH 405 of VA-94, USS *Enterprise* (CVN-65), 1988

Issued to the US Navy on 13 March 1974, this aircraft joined VA-122 at NAS Lemoore two days later. It went on to fly with VA-94, VA-56, VA-27, VA-113, VA-93 and VA-147, before joining VA-94 for a second time on 13 January 1987. After service with the unit, the jet was sent to AMARC for storage on 25 August 1989. In 1995 it was sold through FMS to Thailand, eventually taking up the serial 1409 with No 104 Sqn of the Royal Thai Navy. It was last recorded in storage at U-Tapao Royal Thai Air Base in 2015. The aircraft is depicted here armed with five Mk 83 1000-lb bombs, one each directly attached to pylons at stations 1, 2, 3, 7 and 8, and AIM-9L Sidewinders on cheek stations 4 and 5. The A-7 also carries a 300-gal drop tank on station 6.

25
A-7E BuNo 160537/AC 300 of VA-46, USS *John F Kennedy* (CV-67), 1990-91

Delivered by LTV on 31 January 1977, this aircraft was issued to VA-113 at NAS Lemoore the following day. It moved to Japan to operate with VA-93 in May of that same year, and was exchanged with VA-146 in September 1980. The aircraft returned to Japan once again – and VA-93 – in May 1981. VA-113 took charge of BuNo 160537 for a second time and returned it to Lemoore in September 1982, where it joined VA-122 the following year and VA-22 on 31 January 1985. The A-7 went on to serve with VA-46 from March 1990, and it saw service in Operation *Desert Storm* – the jet was one of eight HARM 'shooters' involved in the Night One attacks on the Baghdad area in the early hours of 17 January 1991, the aircraft being flown by Lt John D Klas. After retirement in the summer of 1991, it was earmarked for FMS sale to Greece as part of a 1992 deal for an additional 50 A-7Es and 18 TA-7Cs. The Corsair II was last recorded as stored at the Greek air base of Araxos in 2014. The aircraft is depicted here in *Desert Storm* Night One configuration, armed with three HARMs on stations 1, 7 and 8 and AIM-9L Sidewinders on cheek stations 4 and 5. It also carries 300-gal drop tanks on stations 3 and 6.

26
A-7E BuNo 160615/AC 310 of VA-46, USS *John F Kennedy* (CV-67), 1990-91

LTV handed this A-7E over to the US Navy on 23 February 1978, and it joined VA-174 the next day. Transferred to VA-46 in 1979, the aircraft subsequently served with VA-15, VA-72, VA-83, VA-86 and VA-105, before being issued to VA-46 once again on 11 August 1990 as the squadron, along with the rest of CVW-3, made preparations to deploy in support of Operation *Desert Shield*, which became *Desert Storm* on 17 January 1991. One of the most uniquely armed carrier aircraft on Night One of the campaign, AC 310, flown by Lt Jeff Greer, carried four TALD ADM-141As mounted two per TER on stations 1 and 8. Designed to fool the enemy's radars into remaining active so they could be destroyed by HARMs, just 137 TALDs were launched during *Desert Storm* by A-7s, A-6s, F/A-18s and S-3s. It is believed that at least one Iraqi interceptor locked onto a TALD, its pilot believing the decoy was a Coalition aircraft, and chased it. One other point of interest for BuNo 160615 is that the aircraft was actually assigned to Lt Greer and carried his name beneath the cockpit. US Navy pilots rarely flew 'their' named aircraft, usually taking whatever was available on the day of their mission. After being struck off charge in the summer of 1991, this jet eventually found its way into private hands and currently rests at the Cavanaugh Flight Museum in Addison, Texas.

27
A-7E BuNo 160552/AC 400 of VA-72, USS *John F Kennedy* (CV-67), 1990-91

Delivered on 18 July 1977 and issued to VA-174 two days later, this aircraft was transferred to VA-72 on 25 October that same year. Unusually, the jet remained with the unit for the rest of its US Navy career. When 'JFK' and CVW-3 deployed in August 1990 for *Desert Shield*, the last two Fleet A-7 squadrons were not sure if they would be flying low-level attacks once in-theatre, as Cdr 'Lites' Leenhouts recalled. 'As I figured that we'd be going low, I thought we should acquire the appropriate paint and camouflage the planes. We ordered water-soluble brown and tan paint and in no time tons of it showed up – during this period, anything and everything that we had ever wanted showed up! However, upon a brief from SPEAR, we were informed that the Iraqis had more than 7000 AAA muzzles out there, so going low wasn't a good idea and we might want to rethink our tactics'. After the war, as CV-67 headed back to CONUS, some of the unused paint was used to mark up AC 400 in camouflage so that it could be photographed during VA-72's fly-off into Cecil Field at the end of the cruise. The remaining paint was then turned over to the ship's disposal department for disposition. Retired by the US Navy in the summer of 1991, BuNo 160552 was sold the following year to the Greek Air Force and served with both 335 and 336 Mira until retirement in October 2014.

28 and 30
A-7E BuNo 158819/AC 402 and 401 of VA-72, USS *John F Kennedy* (CV-67), 1990-91

This aircraft joined VA-174 on 20 April 1973, having been delivered to the US Navy by LTV at the company's Dallas factory the previous day. It transferred to VA-86 on 10 December 1974, serving with that squadron until returning to VA-174 for training duties on 28 September 1977. Following more fleet service with VA-15, it then spent time with VA-82, VA-72 and VA-37, before returning to VA-72 for a second time on 29 September 1989. Although it initially flew as 'Decoy 402' (assigned to Cdr 'Lites' Leenhouts) during Operations *Desert Shield/Desert Storm*, the A-7 was repainted as 'Decoy 401' and duly became the aircraft of squadron CO, Cdr John 'Shooter' Sanders. It remained as such until VA-72 disestablished in May 1991. Today, the jet is preserved at Tillamook, Oregon, in the markings it wore when retired.

29
A-7E BuNo 160714/AC 301 of VA-46, USS *John F Kennedy* (CV-67), 1991
Accepted into service on 24 May 1978, this aircraft was taken on charge by VA-174 six days later. It next served with VA-81,

VA-83, VA-66, VA-72, VA-203, VA-46 and VA-105, before returning to VA-46 on 20 April 1990. This retro scheme was applied after *Desert Storm* had ended, 'Tartan 301's' markings not only incorporating VA-46's impressive mission tally but also the unit's '1955-1991' legend on the fin and the names of select maintenance personnel on the engine exhaust shroud. BuNo 160714 was struck from the inventory on 11 June 1991, and it remains preserved at NAS Pensacola, Florida, as part of the National Naval Aviation Museum.

An A-7E of VA-94 undertakes a dusk patrol over the Northern Arabian Sea in early 1988 (*US Navy*)

INDEX